Christmas 2000

What a nice garden
you have!

with love

Bernard, Lesley, Kirsty,
Jamie & Holly x

THE ROYAL GARDENS IN WINDSOR GREAT PARK

THE ROYAL GARDENS IN WINDSOR GREAT PARK

Charles Lyte

AIDAN ELLIS

For my patient wife, Sarah

First published in the United Kingdom by Aidan Ellis Publishing,
Whinfield, Herbert Road, Salcombe, S Devon TQ8 8HN
First edition 1998

A CIP catalogue record for this book is available from the
British Library
ISBN: 0 85628 261 8

DESIGNED BY CRAIG DODD

Page make-up and typesetting by the Midlands Book
Typesetting Company, Loughborough, Leics LE11 1HH
Text film and colour reproduction by DP Graphics, Trowbridge,
Wilts BA14 6DN
Printed in Spain

Half-title: Rh. veitchianum (Cubitii Group) 'Ashcome' FCC
Frontispiece: Spring cascade: *Wisteria sinensis*
Title page: Rh. orbiculare x 'Richard Gill'
Opposite: Camellia 'Inspiration'

CONTENTS

Acknowledgements

Researching and writing *The Royal Gardens in Windsor Great Park* has been one of the most absorbing and enjoyable experiences of my life, made all the better by an enormous amount of help and enthusiasm.

My particular thanks go to John Bond, L.V.O., V.M.H., the outstanding post-war Keeper of the Gardens, who gave up a great deal of his time to showing me the gardens, and for checking through my manuscript. I am also enormously grateful to the Hon. Mrs. Roberts, Curator of the Print Room, Royal Library, Windsor Castle, who was unstinting in her help and advice, generously allowed me to make use of her superbly researched manuscript of *The History and Buildings of the Home Park and the Great Park at Windsor*, and for reading and correcting my own manuscript. I would also like to thank Dr. Brent Elliott and his staff at the Royal Horticultural Society Lindley Library for their help in my researches; the staff of the Savill and Valley Gardens who answered my many questions, and to Roy Lancaster and Tony Schilling for helping me identify the plants they have collected which are growing in the gardens. And, of course, my grateful thanks to Sir Simon Hornby, President of the Royal Horticultural Society, for his foreword.

Last, but by no means least, a very special thanks to Tim Sandall, for his wonderful photography, for being such an excellent colleague, and a fine companion on our safaris round the gardens

Charles Lyte

Photographic credits: The photographs were all taken by Tim Sandall, except for the following: The Royal Collection © Her Majesty The Queen, pages 22, 24, 25; John Bond, pages 19, 50, 56, 62, 69, 76, 80, 83, 94, 98, 116, 139, 145, 146, 157(*top*), 158 (*top*), 160, 164/65, 170, 172, 173, 175, 178, 182, 191; David Hartley, page 54 (*left*); Mastertag, pages 20, 58, 90, 112, 151; Lyn Randall, pages 51, 53, 54 (*above*), 71, 148 (*bottom*), 166, 169, 179; Royal Horticultural Society, page 41; Savill Garden Collection, page 124; Beric Tempest, pages contents, 49, 72, 74, 103

Following pages: A Winter Scene, Savill Garden; The Upper Pond in late spring, Savill Garden; Confetti!, Savill Garden; Autumn glory, Valley Gardens

Foreword

I first visited the Savill gardens in 1950; my mother and I climbed over some rickety steps to reach the secret paradise of the bog garden (as it was then). I remember on my first visit being bowled over by the fields of wild narcissus and the early magnolias, and then in May, finding drifts of candelabra primulas and the blue meconopsis with the great yellow and white lysichitons lining the stream.

Over the years, I have been back at different times of the year to get inspiration and to learn from the huge collection of trees and shrubs which has been brought to the Windsor gardens, planted with such care and nurtured with such skill.

In March 1997, I spent an afternoon with John Bond going round the Valley and Savill Gardens. I can't ever remember getting such pure joy from a garden. The season had brought flowers in profusion; the magnolias were magnificent, all shades of pink and white soaring up into the clear blue sky, surrounded by camellias, rhododendrons and pieris, unusually all flowering together, as if determined to give John Bond, in his final spring, a resounding farewell. I rang up my gardening friends telling them to drop everything and go to Windsor Park for I knew that they were unlikely ever again to see such a brilliant display.

The Windsor Gardens are a triumph of good gardening. In sixty-five years there have been two remarkable men responsible for making and developing these gardens. Eric Savill, the visionary and designer, and John Bond, the gardener, who has built the collection and nurtured the plants with such love and skill.

This excellent book describes the great beauty hidden in Windsor Park. I hope it makes many more people visit them; they won't see better gardening on such a grand scale anywhere else in Britain.

Sir Simon Hornby
President of the Royal Horticultural Society

INTRODUCTION

A medley of dwarf daffodils

When the course of the River Thames was pushed south by the glaciers of the Ice Age over two million years ago, it proved to be more than just a part of the evolutionary process; it was an important step towards an extraordinary enclave in British history – Windsor and its forest. In those incredibly ancient times England was physically joined to northern Europe, and mammoths, woolly rhinoceros, wild ox, elephants, hippos, deer, bison, musk-ox, lions, reindeer, wild pigs and cats, horses and beaver lumbered, wallowed, grazed and hunted in the lush and tropical Thames Valley, while the river itself was little more than a tributary of the River Rhine. By a nice coincidence it is very probable that magnolias and rhododendrons, or their very close relatives, bloomed close to where they now flourish in the Valley and Savill Gardens in Windsor Great Park and in the royal gardens of Frogmore and Royal Lodge, along another tributary of the same river.

Eventually the convulsions of the planet prised Britain apart from the rest of Europe, and the Thames, quite a modest little river in continental European terms, became a defensive ditch valued by successive rulers and monarchs attempting to establish control of the island, and the chance to create dynasties, not always very successfully.

Three hundred thousand years before Christ, Paleolithic tribes of the Acheulian hand-axe culture hunted and fished in the Thames Valley. They were followed by Neolithic farmers, Iberians, Celts, Gauls, Romans, Saxons, Danes and Normans. Celts established colonies, but it was the Saxon kings who built a settlement at what is now Old Windsor, which gave them easy access to the river as a highway of communication, and the rich hunting fields of the neighbouring forest. It was also a strategically useful place, but not so defensible as the high ground where Windsor Castle now stands, first built as a fort by William the Conqueror.

The Great Park was carved out of the vast area to the south of the Thames in Norman times for conserving deer, which were hunted in the forest and where it is possible that there were still wild boar at that time. It was written of William's passion for hunting that he '. . . loved the tall game (deer) as if he had been their father'.

When it became a park in its own right, the Great Park not only contained considerable herds of deer, but also had managed rabbit warrens, and its streams were dammed to create fish pools. The purpose of the park was to supply food for the castle as well as sport, and indeed the keepers had to grow hay around their cottages for winter fodder for the deer.

The old forest stretched north to south through Sunningdale, bisecting the area now occupied by Virginia Water to form the eastern border. Where the River Lodden from Hampshire enters the Thames a mile above Wargrave was the western border, with the Blackwater marking the southern boundary; a polyhedron with irregular sides, within which are now Windsor Castle, the Great and the Home Parks, the Savill and the Valley Gardens, Frogmore, Royal Lodge and Virginia Water.

Windsor Forest abounds with legends. One is that one of King Arthur's most famous knights, Sir Launcelot du Lac, went to stay with a hermit, Sir Brastias, who lived in the forest, to prepare for a great tournament. One day he was relaxing by the spring at the hermitage when a renowned lady huntress galloped into the clearing after a deer, shot at it, missed the animal, but pierced Launcelot in the backside, apologised and rode on.

While the popular image of a forest is vast acres of trees, in fact it really means a wild, uncultivated wilderness, and this was certainly true of Windsor Forest, much of which was bleak, windswept, intimidating sandy heath. In the reign of George I, Daniel Defoe wrote this chilling description:

'. . . here is a vast tract of land, some of it within seventeen or eighteen miles of the capital city; which is not only poor, but even quite steril (sic), given up to barrenness, horrid and frightful to look on, not only good for little, but good for nothing; much of it is a sandy desert, and one may frequently be put in mind here of Arabia Deserta, where the winds raise the sands, so as to overwhelm whole caravans of travellers, cattle and people together.'

The Great Park started to become a definitive area within Windsor Forest in the 1240s in the reign of King Henry III. Both the Great Park and the smaller area of parkland around the castle, now known as the Home Park, were established by the end of the fourteenth century. By 1607 it was estimated that the area of the Great Park was 3,650 acres. Now it is 4,800 acres.

Until the establishment of the Commonwealth following the Civil War, like all parks and forests from the Middle Ages, Windsor Forest was royal. Following the temporary destruction of the monarchy what is now the Great Park, and a lot more land, was sold off by Parliament to pay the army, which had all but wiped out the deer – Cromwell kept the Little Park for hunting. The lands returned fully to crown ownership after the Restoration in 1660.

The diarist and arboriculturist, John Evelyn – he wrote the classic work *Sylva* in 1678 – was quite a frequent visitor to Windsor. On 23 October 1686, when he was there, he noted in his diary:

'The ground is clayey and moist: the water stark nought; the park is pretty; . . .'

William Cobbett, the great liberal reformer and agronomist, was not a man to mince his words. Crossing the Windsor Park on horseback on his way to Reading on 9 November 1822, he recorded in his famous *Rural Rides*:

'Started at day-break in a hazy frost, for Reading. The horses' manes and ears covered with the hoar before we got across Windsor Park, which appeared to be a blackguard soil, pretty much like Hounslow Heath, only not flat. A very large part of the Park is covered with heath or rushes, sure sign of execrable soil.' However, he approved of the roads, which he thought must have been made by a Solomon. 'I am but a traveller; and the roads in this park are beautiful indeed.'

In fact the Great Park is not just a 'blackguard soil'. It is made up of at least two distinct types – a heavy loam in the northern part, sandy hills and dales in the southern, broken up by ponds and lakes, and large areas of matted turf.

From the time of the Conqueror, and no doubt the Saxon kings before, the main royal sporting pastime was hunting, and none were more enthusiastic than the Tudors and Stuarts.

Rh. kiusianum in association w
Rh. x *loderi*

The sweet-scented *Rh. luteum*

It was the Hanoverians who began the changes which have now made the parks places of outstanding beauty, building royal homes whose legacy is Royal Lodge and Frogmore, and, of course, the unique Savill and Valley Gardens, with their huge collections of plants.

The national and other major plant collections in the two gardens are outstanding – three hundred and ninety-nine species and cultivars of ferns; four hundred and forty-four species and cultivars of acers; two thousand, two hundred and twenty rhododendron species and hybrids; one hundred and eighty-seven Glenn Dale azalea cultivars; one hundred and forty-two Knaphill azalea cultivars; fifty-two beech (fagus) species and cultivars; two hundred and six oak (quercus) species and cultivars; three hundred and fifty-one birch (betula) species and cultivars; eighty-five sorbus (aucuparia section), two thousand, five hundred and twenty-one conifer species and cultivars; three hundred and sixteen magnolia species and cultivars; ninety mahonia species and cultivars; one hundred and twenty pieris species and cultivars; three hundred and nineteen holly (ilex) species and cultivars; twenty-nine skimmia species and cultivars; six hundred and eighty-five heather species and cultivars, and two hundred and seventy-one hosta species and cultivars.

Even this enormous collection does not represent the full extent of the plants grown in the gardens, but what it does say is that the royal gardens of Windsor Great Park are unique and magnificent creations.

The Great Park is not only home to outstanding gardens, but also to a large diversity of wild life. The oaks are the source of food for two hundred and eighty insect species, and there are over two thousand varieties of beetles in the park, which is more than half the total for the entire British Isles.

Among the many birds are warblers, greater spotted, lesser spotted and green woodpeckers, nuthatch, redstart, tree creeper, woodlark, sparrowhawk, stonechat, nightjar and finches. Hawfinch are attracted to the gardens by the abundance of berries.

Virginia Water and the ponds support mandarin, mallard, teal, shoveller, pochard, widgeon, shelduck, tufted ducks and Canada geese.

A large range of fungi are to be found in the woodland, as well as wild flowers, butterflies and moths.

THE BEGINNING OF PARADISE

Top: Scene on the Virginia Water by Daniell

Bottom: The Cascade and Grotto: from Eight Views of Windsor Great Park by Paul Sandby and E. Rooker

The translation of the word for a garden in ancient Persian is 'paradise', for to the Persians a garden should represent man's concept of paradise – a place of infinite beauty, peace and pleasure.

When he was appointed Ranger of the Park in 1746, William, Duke of Cumberland, second son of George II, began the work of transforming the bleakness of Windsor Great Park into a place of exceptional beauty. What he started was to take over two hundred years to bring to its present state with the Savill and Valley Gardens, and the gardens attached to Royal Lodge.

It might seem an extraordinary thing that a man whose military career earned him the vile soubriquet of 'Butcher' Cumberland after he destroyed the Jacobite rebellion at Cullodon in a terrible slaughter, and followed it up by the bloody and merciless pursuit of the rebels, should then, just a year later, in 1746, turn his energies towards the transformation of the park.

In fact he had been involved with Windsor through his hunting lodge near Bracknell for some years, and while his brother, Frederick, Prince of Wales, did his best to blacken his reputation, Cumberland was an inspired patron of the arts – and of gardening. Not only did he engage in a considerable programme of planting forest trees, but created his greatest single memorial, the first Virginia Water, which was a good deal smaller than the present three hundred-acre lake.

The first attempt at creating this now famous stretch of water, which has had such a huge influence on the creation of the Valley Gardens, was not a lasting success. The original pondhead was destroyed by a deluge of rain in 1768, and was rebuilt in the 1780s. Thomas Sandby, who with his brother Paul, left a superb record of eighteenth century Windsor in their fine water-colours of the castle and the buildings and views of the Great Park, was closely involved with the rebuilding.

Fed by quite a small stream known as the Windles, although there is some doubt that it really was the Windles, and also as Virginia or Virginy River – there is an unsubstantiated legend that it was named after the Virgin Queen, Queen Elizabeth I – Virginia Water, and the Obelisk Pond and Great Meadow Pond are said to have been built by the labour of the duke's army, which he had raised to destroy the Jacobites. Such back-breaking hard labour seems a poor reward for having fought for the duke and brought him acclaim. However, not so far away is Breakheart Hill, now part of the Valley Gardens, where there is supposed to have been a prisoner-of-war camp for captive Jacobites and later French prisoners-of-war. It might seem logical that prisoners were used in the work, but there is no evidence that they were.

The duke's other contributions were the pleasure grounds and kitchen gardens at the Great (now Cumberland) Lodge. The most obvious memorial to him is the

Design for the East End of Virginia Water by Sandby

dominant obelisk in the open parkland which was raised on the orders of his father to mark his military achievements.

Virginia Water was the main focus for royal activity in the Great Park, with the building of Fort Belvedere in 1755 by Cumberland's nephew, Henry, who succeeded to the title and the rangership. George III completed the great lake, built the present waterfall and planted a large range of trees – pine, larch, spruce, acacia, acer, horse chestnut, hornbeam, holm oak (*Quercus ilex*), cedar of Lebanon and sweet chestnut on the northern heights above the water.

George IV had part of the ruins of a two thousand-year-old temple, which had been brought to this country from Leptis Magna, the Roman city near Tripoli in Libya, erected by Virginia Water to 'beautify his garden'. He also built the exotic

fishing lodge on the edge of the lake, which was used for angling parties and general jollification. William IV had a scaled down frigate on the water to satisfy his urge to command a fighting vessel of his own.

Windsor Castle did not attract the same royal enthusiasm for gardening. It did not lend itself greatly to garden making, although there are charming features like the east terrace garden formed by George IV in the 1820s, and the stream garden.

Frogmore and Royal Lodge are the two private royal gardens which bear the distinctive mark put on them over the years by their royal occupants.

FROGMORE

'orm and foliage: a marginal lanting in the Savill Garden

)verleaf: Frogmore House

Frogmore is on extremely low-lying ground, virtually on a level with the River Thames, and was prone to flooding. The name, in fact, means frog lake or pool. Despite that, the land has been occupied since the fourteenth century, and is mentioned in Shakespeare's *Merry Wives of Windsor.* It was eventually to become a favourite place of refuge for the Widow of Windsor, Queen Victoria, where she particularly enjoyed the gardens, visiting them almost daily when she was in residence in Windsor Castle.

Before becoming crown property in 1550, it belonged to a family called Avelyn, and was known as Avelyns, and until it passed into the hands of the Parliamentary Commissioners after the Civil War, it was leased by a number of different tenants. The Commissioners sold the property to the governor of Windsor Castle, a Colonel Whichcote, for two thousand, eight hundred pounds. After the Restoration it was handed back to the Crown.

By this time the estate had fallen into a sad state of disrepair, and remained so until leased to a family called Aldworth, who began building a new house during the late seventeenth century. That house forms the core of the present Frogmore house. As well as house builders they were great tree planters, a tradition that was to be continued with enthusiasm by Queen Victoria.

The Aldworth family left the estate in 1700 when the lease was transferred to George Fitzroy, Duke of Northumberland, the youngest son of Charles II and the Duchess of Cleveland. Following the duke's death his widow stayed in residence, and at her death the lease passed to her niece, Grace Parsons, whose trustees sublet the property to a succession of tenants, including Sir Robert Walpole's second son, Edward. In the early 1790s the crown lease was acquired for Queen Charlotte, wife of George III. While the queen continued to live with the rest of the royal family at Queen's Lodge or in Windsor Castle, the land attached to Frogmore served as the ideal pleasure grounds.

For the gardens of Frogmore, the arrival of Queen Charlotte was a turning point. She and her daughters, the Princesses Amelia, Augusta and Elizabeth made their lives there.

To start with they concentrated on Little Frogmore, previously Frogmore Farm, which was renamed Amelia Cottage, after the queen's daughter. The architect James Wyatt designed a Gothic cottage to replace the farmhouse, but this scheme was abandoned when the two separate estates at Frogmore, Great Frogmore and Little Frogmore, were merged into one estate in 1792.

Queen Charlotte, who became George III's wife, and queen, on the clear understanding that she kept out of politics and public affairs, found she had plenty to occupy her in producing fifteen children, of whom thirteen survived, and a consuming passion for plants and gardening. When she lived at Kew she developed her natural talent for botany, but it was at Frogmore that she turned her considerable energies to gardening, in which she involved her daughters.

She engaged the leading gardeners of the day to make, as she described it '. . . this unpritty (sic) thing pritty (sic)'. Greatly influenced by the picturesque style and Marie Antoinette's Petit Trianon at Versailles, she built temples, Gothic ruins, a thatched barn for dancing and a cornmill. Only the Gothic ruins remain, and they were allowed to fall into such a bad state of disrepair, which sounds odd for ruins, that they had to be virtually rebuilt at the beginning of the present century.

Mounts were thrown up, winding walks laid down. Water was confined in canals. A temporary pageant temple was built for the queen by Wyatt in 1809 on the spot now occupied by the tempietto built for Queen Victoria's mother, the Duchess of Kent. It was from this domed building that the queen supervised her spectacular entertainments.

As well as the picturesque architecture of the garden, Queen Charlotte planted it with a rich diversity of plants mainly drawn from Kew – *Rhododendron ponticum* and *Rh. periclymenoides*; spirea; hydrangeas; daphnes; magnolias; clematis; cyclamen; geraniums; violas; hyacinths and anemones. Additionally there were bright beds of flowers.

Entirely artificial, it was laid out to create sharply differing moods from Gothic gloom to midsummer brilliance. But it must have come to life in the most theatrical manner when the queen threw a party, which was something she enjoyed doing practically until her death. Her last big fête was in July 1817 – she died at the age of seventy-four on 17 November 1818 – when she invited two thousand guests, including five hundred boys from nearby Eton College, who played a cricket match on the lawn.

Frogmore was left to Charlotte's daughter, Princess Augusta, under whom it became a residence once again. She continued gardening, adding a conservatory for her collection of geraniums (pelargoniums), cactus, stocks, verbena, azaleas and a large myrtle tree, and a camellia house, which also accommodated South African ericas. The Duchess of Kent, Queen Victoria's mother, who was the next to occupy the estate, added a vinery. However, in the years following Queen Charlotte's death the garden must have gone into something of a decline if we are to believe Prince Puckler-Muskau, who, on a visit in 1827, described the gardens as 'a remarkably dull place'.

When the Duchess of Kent died her body was entombed in a mausoleum designed by Prince Albert. It was a portent that this historic garden would become, in part at least, a royal cemetery, for when the prince consort died on 14 December 1861, the queen ordered the building of the great mausoleum in the south-west part of the garden, where she lies with the prince, with the graves of other royalty in the level lawn outside. With the preponderance of evergreens planted in the queen's lifetime it is as though the garden was put into mourning, and even to this day it is possible to clearly detect in the grounds the depth of despair and grief at the loss of her prince consort.

The mausoleum is a building of some magnificence. In the form of a Greek Cross, it is built in the Italian Romanesque style which gives it a Mediterranean Catholic look. However it was constructed of materials that clearly reflected both the British Isles and the might of the British Empire: marble from Wales and Ireland; granite from

Friends' Summer House, Savil
Garden

The Tea House

Scotland, the Channel Islands, Devon and Cornwall; serpentine from Cornwall; Portland stone from the south; teak from India, and copper for the roof from Australia. The queen's close family ties with Europe were represented by marble for the interior from Belgium, France, Italy, Greece and Portugal.

Having built the mausoleum the queen then tried to bury it in a forest of conifers. The main plantings, all by royalty of Europe and Russia, began in earnest in 1864. Visiting members of these royal families were wise to bring their gardening boots and a spade on a visit to Frogmore for they were sure to be expected to plant a tree. (Appendix A)

The majority of the trees planted were, in the nineteenth century, regarded as memorial trees because of their longevity, but the Veitch *A Manual of the Coniferae*, published in 1881, states: 'None of them, however, will fulfil the object of a Memorial Tree in the immediate vicinity of large towns. The antipathy of the whole Order to the influence of smoke is irremediable.' This, perhaps, explains why so few of the trees are to be found round the mausoleum today. However, there is a magnificent London plane (*Platanus* x *acerifolia*) close to the building, and that is a tree impervious to atmospheric pollution.

All was not gloom at Frogmore in Queen Victoria's time. The shrubs still flowered as they do today. There were roses and Ghent azaleas, and ivy basket beds planted with spring and summer bedding. The Indian kiosk taken by Lord Canning from Lucknow added an exotic touch.

There is one small part of the thirty-five-acre garden that seems, to me at least, most alive with the presence of Queen Victoria, and that is her little tea house, with its scalloped tiles and Tudor-style chimneys. Just outside are two holm oaks (*Quercus ilex*) with massive, spreading boles. The queen, attended by her splendidly uniformed and turbaned Indian servant, Chidda, worked on her state papers on the lawn in the shade of the trees.

The tea house is unchanged. The timber is painted the same sombre olive green colour she chose; the hand-painted wallpaper, the simple furniture, the photograph of herself, Prince Albert and their children, and one of her with John Brown, her gillie, are as they were in her lifetime.

Connected to the house is the tiny kitchen with its minute range and lead-lined sink where the teas were prepared and cleared away.

Sadly not all that was part of the gardens of Frogmore has withstood the depredation of time. One of its most spectacular features, the great fifty-acre kitchen garden, is reduced to a remnant. Although part of the neighbouring Shaw Estate, the kitchen garden was clearly closely allied to the Victorian royal gardening scene.

In a lengthy article in *The Journal of Horticulture: Cottage Gardener and Home Farmer* in 1897, the Royal Supply Gardens at Frogmore, as they were rather mundanely named, were described thus:

'Everything that a well-appointed, well-equipped, and well-managed garden can be made to yield is provided here, and transmitted to wherever the Queen and Court may be in residence, whether at the Castle, Buckingham Palace, Balmoral, Osborne, the South of France or elsewhere. Packing may be said to be always in progress.' For state occasions at Buckingham Palace, or wherever the court was, a special train was chartered to carry the flowering and foliage plants, and produce, needed. Prior to the creation of the kitchen garden, produce for the royal establishments was grown at about half a dozen different locations, including Kew, Hampton Court, Kensington Palace and Cumberland Lodge.

The site chosen for Victoria's kitchen garden was in the Home Park immediately below Frogmore House pleasure gardens. It was on heavy marl, damp, often blanketed in fog and something of a frost pocket, not, one would have thought, the ideal location for a garden that would have to produce huge quantities of vegetables, fruit, pot plants and cut flowers. The first garden was of thirty-one acres enclosed within a twelve-foot wall. The area was later extended to fifty acres. It cost fifty thousand pounds to construct, about two and a half million pounds in modern money.

The statistics for the garden are fascinating, even mind-boggling. It is worth mentioning some of them here. (Appendix B)

About five thousand pounds of grapes were harvested from eleven vineries where Black Hamburg and Foster's Seedling were grown for an early crop, followed by Madresfield Court, Golden Champion and Duke of Buccleuch, with the late crop coming from Muscat of Alexandria, Black Alicante, Gros Colman, Lady Downe's, West's St. Peter's and Raisin de Calabre. Pineapples from the pine pits – Smooth Cayenne and Charlotte Rothschild – averaged seven and a half pounds per fruit. In addition to hot bed pits, six melon houses growing Frogmore Orange, Royal Favourite and The Lady produced five hundred and fifty fruits a year.

Strawberries were in season the year round from seven thousand plants of La Grosse Sucre, Royal Sovereign and Vicomtesse Hericart de Thury outside, and another ten thousand for forcing. Starting in February a minimum of ten pounds a day were picked, going up to three hundred and fifty pounds a month at the height of the season. Wherever the queen was, whether Windsor, the Isle of Wight, Buckingham Palace, Balmoral or the south of France, strawberries were sent to her. La Grosse Sucre was grown specially for Balmoral as it stood the six hundred-mile train journey well.

Because they were the queen's particular favourite there had to be a fairly constant supply of cherries. A span-roofed glass house running north and south contained seventy pyramid-trained Belle d'Orleans, Early Rivers, May Duke, Governor Wood, Frogmore Bigarreau and Black Tartarian for the earliest crop.

This huge kitchen garden, with an average of a man to an acre – every year a few acres were trenched by hand two and a half to three feet deep and heavily manured – had to feed, at Windsor Castle alone, three hundred people a day, so along with the fruit, the vegetable production was prodigious.

There were four one hundred-yard-long asparagus beds covering three acres, and twenty thousand seakale crowns. Early potatoes were grown in leaf-mould in heated pits, and seventy tons of maincrop were harvested from Dunbar, Regent and Fortyfold.

As well as supplying the Royal Household with vegetables and fruit wherever the court was, Victoria's great kitchen garden had to grow over three thousand boxes of cut flowers for decoration, plus enough to make up crosses and wreathes for an apparently endless succession of funerals.

Ornamental plants for Buckingham Palace, Windsor Castle, Balmoral and Osborne were raised under glass. There were also palms, bananas and bamboos, fuchsias, begonias, poinsettias, variegated eulalias (*Miscanthus sinensis*), and two thousand, five hundred chrysanthemum plants.

The orchid houses were spectacular with their collections of cattleyas, cypripediums, oncidiums, lycastes, *Peristeria elata* and coelogynes.

Frogmore pleasure gardens are a great deal more modest now than in Queen Victoria's time, but they still have the grace and charm that was such a comfort to her. There are fine and interesting trees like the fastigiate form of the English oak (*Quercus robur*), magnificent examples of the tulip tree (*Liriodendron tulipifera*), and the Himalayan pine (*Pinus wallichiana*), and two splendid 'Dawyck' beeches – the fastigiate form of the common beech (*Fagus sylvatica*), which were planted in 1934 by the then Duke of Kent.

On a royal scale is the half-mile-long mixed border. There are lime trees (tilia) clotted with mistletoe; ornamental cherries, beds of Pemberton musk roses; great drifts of spring bulbs – Queen Mary had a lot to do with them; flowering shrubs, and the evergreens that give the gardens their distinctive Victorian atmosphere.

Rosa 'Climbing Cécile Brunner' and *Fremontodendron* 'California Glory' on the wall, Savill Garden

ROYAL LODGE

Azalea tapestry

Stand on the long terrace of Royal Lodge, the Berkshire home of Queen Elizabeth, the Queen Mother, and look out across the sloping lawns fringed by the woodland garden and beyond to open English countryside, and it is impossible to believe that you are only twenty miles from Hyde Park Corner and the heart of London. The only hint is the aircraft climbing out of and descending into Heathrow Airport, which is even closer. Take those away and you are standing outside a fine country house in a good English garden.

The overwhelming impression is that here is a family home and garden, and it is the right impression, because in 1931, when they accepted the offer of the house from King George V, the Duke and Duchess of York – later King George VI and Queen Elizabeth – set out to achieve just that, and succeeded in doing so. In their hands it became a place of charm, grace and tranquillity, very unlike the capricious, but not unattractive management it underwent when it was occupied by the prince regent, later George IV.

Royal Lodge does not have the long history of Frogmore, and while doubtless the land had been settled and in use one way or another for a considerable time, the first record of a house was not made until 1662, following the Restoration. Then it was known as Watkins House. Nine years later it was called Garden House or Gardener's House. Nearly eighty years later it was named The Dairy and, alternatively, Dairy House, and was surrounded by an acre of enclosed land. Despite the simplicity of its name, it was by now quite a substantial building, and was occupied by senior royal servants, the most distinguished being Thomas Sandby, who was appointed steward to the Duke of Cumberland, which made him effectively Deputy Ranger of Windsor Great Park.

After Thomas Sandby's death, the bailiff in the Great Park, Joseph Frost, moved in. Before long George III took a brief interest in the house; however, that came to nothing.

The original idea was for the house to serve as temporary accommodation for the prince regent while work on Cumberland Lodge was being completed.

Needless to say the Dairy House was too simple for the royal family. Additional rooms were needed, such as an eating room, a gallery and a conservatory, as well as a verandah on the east and south sides. All of this came at a time when a romantic ideal of a simple rural life was all the vogue, and with it the cottage orné – a notion which later was perpetuated by the nineteenth century and early twentieth century paintings of Helen Allingham, Myles Birket Foster and William Stephen Coleman, but not one borne out by real rural cottage existence.

Once the charm of 'cottage life' had taken root with the prince regent he set out on a programme of changes to the building which was to transform it into historically the largest cottage ever built. He brought in John Nash, the architect of his gorgeous Brighton Pavilion, and between them they wrought the work of transformation, which must have been like witnessing a caterpillar turning into a chrysalis, and emerging as a brilliantly painted butterfly.

The first cottage effect was a thatched roof. That was short-lived and was torn off to be replaced with slates. When the regent became king, the house was considerably enlarged with new rooms, including a billiard room and a dining-room on a scale suitable for royal entertaining.

Jeffry Wyatt, nephew of James Wyatt, architect to George III, took over from John Nash as the improvements and additions proceeded. The commission seems to have turned his head, because he decided that he should enrich his name with the addition of 'ville'. Could he add 'ville' to Wyatt, he asked the king, who replied:

'Veal or mutton, call yourself what you like.'

Despite the royal quip, the relationship between Wyatt and the prince regent was a good one.

After the accession of George IV to the throne, a programme of costly works and improvements to Windsor Castle was begun. They ran into hundreds of thousands of pounds. While they were in progress the king spent more time at Royal Lodge, which he furnished with perfect, but extravagant taste. Gradually he transferred the finest paintings in his collection from Carlton House to the lodge.

Clearly he loved it as much as he did his Royal Pavilion in Brighton, and it was at Royal Lodge that he enjoyed throwing parties. The Duke of Wellington commented, rather disapprovingly, it seems, that it was 'in a constant state of Junketting'. Queen Victoria, as a young princess, was entertained there.

As well as the building and its contents, the king took great pride in the gardens, beginning with his conservatory, which was filled with choice and rare plants, to the massive plantings of trees and shrubs to create vistas and views, as well as provide the privacy that he cherished in later life as a protection against the growing tide of criticism against him. George IV's cottage orné was not to last. After his death the greater part of it was demolished. All that was left of its former magnificence was the great dining-room. However, the materials were not wasted. They were used in other developments around the Windsor crown lands, including adding rooms to an enchanting house in the Home Park called Adelaide Cottage. What was left of Royal Lodge was saved from complete ruin by the prince consort, Prince Albert, who had it repaired as a home for his private secretary, George Anson.

Later it was suggested that Queen Victoria and her consort should use it as a country house, but they rejected the idea, although her second son, eleven-year-old Alfred, Duke of Edinburgh, was installed in it with a tutor so that he could study undisturbed.

From 1865 it was used partly as a kind of grace and favour house, and partly to accommodate various courtiers.

By 1931 it was again in a seriously rundown condition, but not so bad that King George V did not think that it could be restored for the use of his second son, the Duke of York (later King George VI) and his young wife, Elizabeth. After visiting it in the September of that year, the duke wrote to his father: 'It is too kind of you to have offered us Royal Lodge & now having seen it I think it will suit us admirably.' And so

THE SAVILL GARDEN

:ool and green in summer

After the creation of the fishing island and the gardens of Frogmore and Royal Lodge there was a long pause in garden development in Windsor Great Park, and, indeed, there might never have been any but for the vision and innate talent for garden creation of one man, then Eric Savill, later Sir Eric, the Deputy Ranger and Deputy Surveyor of Windsor Great Park and the Windsor Estate.

Eric Savill was, by profession, a land agent and a farmer, two invaluable talents which were linked to a great love of plants and gardening. His father was Sir Edwin Savill, the head of the London firm of land agents and chartered surveyors, Alfred Savill & Sons, and following the family tradition, Eric joined the firm in 1920 after coming down from Magdalene College, Cambridge. His university career was interrupted when he joined up to fight in the First World War – he was badly wounded during the Battle of the Somme in 1916 – but resumed after the war. The discipline he chose was agriculture and estate management.

Six years after joining the family firm he became a partner, and his future seemed to be clearly mapped out, and probably would have been set in concrete but for a Cambridge friendship with a fellow undergraduate, Owen, later Sir Owen, Morshead, with whom he shared lodgings. Eventually Morshead became the librarian of Windsor Castle, and when he was working in London Eric frequently spent weekends with Owen and his family. Much of the time during those peaceful breaks was spent walking in the Great Park along the woodland rides laid out by George II, George III and George IV, and by the side of Virginia Water, the site of the Valley Gardens. The magnificent ancient beeches and oaks enchanted him.

After eleven years working for Alfred Savill & Sons, quite unexpectedly he was offered the post of Deputy Surveyor of Windsor Parks and Woods by the Crown Commissioners, involving looking after fifteen thousand acres, which included forest and farmland. Although he was abandoning a lucrative partnership, the love he had developed for Windsor Great Park won the day. Six years after taking up the appointment he additionally became deputy ranger. His influence on the ancient royal estate was to be as profound, perhaps more so, than monarchs and menials who had gone before him.

While the Windsor Estate is technically the property of the monarch – the Queen holds the title-deeds – it is administered by the Crown Commissioners, which is a government department financed by the national treasury for the ruler of the day, which is one reason why so many of its properties are accessible to the public. When Savill took over the estate there were the woodlands, Virginia Water and boggy dells and valleys, but no garden plantings whatsoever, except great thickets of *Rhododendron ponticum*. Frogmore and Royal Lodge were not accessible to the public. He believed that the creation of a woodland garden would have great popular appeal, and he had the vision to recognise that the terrain of the park, and the availability of natural water, were perfect for creating an important garden.

Magnolia sprengeri 'Eric Savill'

The site Sir Eric settled upon was on the east side of the park close to Englefield Green, the childhood home of the plant collector, Frank Kingdon-Ward, many of whose rhododendron discoveries in Asia are growing in the Savill and Valley Gardens. It was a tangled jungle of *Rhododendron ponticum*, bracken, brambles, elder and laurel. So dense was the growth that there was no visual evidence of the stream which now feeds the ponds in the garden. It was a safe haven for pigeons, rabbits, foxes and pheasants, and it was boggy.

Such a dauntingly overgrown site would have put off lesser men, but Sir Eric had the drive that ignored problems and difficulties, and the ruthlessness to shape and mould nature to his purpose. He also had powerful and enthusiastic supporters in King George V and Queen Mary, the Prince of Wales, briefly King Edward VIII, later the Duke of Windsor, who during his gardening days at Fort Belvedere became an expert on rhododendrons, and the Duke and Duchess of York, later King George VI and Queen Elizabeth, who were then developing their garden at Royal Lodge. All of them were knowledgeable and enthusiastic gardeners and, once persuaded, gave the creation of a woodland garden in the Great Park their full backing.

Indeed, it was George VI, who, on 7 July 1951, decreed that the woodland or bog gardens, as they were then known, should be called the Savill Garden, in perpetual honour of the man who created it.

Work on carving the garden out of the wilderness began in the winter of 1932, marked daily by huge bonfires of undergrowth. At the same time the area was enclosed by a rabbit-proof fence.

By the end of the winter the north-east end of the garden had been opened up and a ditch dug to drain the bogland and form a narrow stream.

The following winter the Upper Pond site was cleared and dammed to form a sheet of water, fed by the stream, which looks as though it has been there since the beginning of time. It is where mallard and Canada geese raise their broods, and huge carp bask and feed with satisfied sucking sounds.

Where there had once been a tangle of growth, now there was water, and the clear form of the gardens emerging from the wilderness, but there was no serious planting. One plant that Sir Eric particularly wanted for the pond and stream sides were kingcups (*Caltha palustris*). The then park foreman, Harry Wye, heard of this, and bartered snared rabbits for a basketful of plants; the ancestors of the clumps that have naturalised by the water. With so many natural habitats for these lovely native plants having been lost to land drainage and modern farming methods, the Windsor kingcups, at least, are safe.

For a short while rabbits were used as a currency for obtaining plants, but not for long. As the garden developed there was a growing stream of gifts, and as these and others were propagated at the garden, so a tradition of exchange with private, public and botanic gardens was developed, and it continues today.

Savill Garden and its sibling, the Valley Gardens, play a vital role in sustaining a vast collection running into many thousands of species, hybrids and cultivars of trees, shrubs, and herbaceous perennials.

Since the Second World War about five hundred rhododendron hybrids have been

Above: Alpines on raised beds

Left: Her Majesty the Queen with John Bond

from the pond to withering shrubs and trees. After that a permanent grid irrigation system was installed.

In the early days the garden was essentially planted for the spring, which is a natural style for a woodland garden, but it became increasingly important to attract visitors throughout the year, or at least throughout the main seasons. This led to the development of special features, such as the now famous herbaceous borders on either side of the wide green walk, presided over by a magnificent willow-leaf podocarp (*Podocarpus salignus*) from southern Chile. Although it looks like one huge tree, it is in fact a cluster of trees, resulting from a tray of seedlings left in what was then a nursery area, which eventually rooted themselves through the tray – an oversight that has proved to be a beautiful feature.

A Michaelmas daisy (aster) bed was planted, and peony and rose borders, lilies, and trees and shrubs for autumn colour and fruit.

Roses were grown behind the herbaceous border, but this area has now been remade as a Dry Garden with a wide range of drought-resistant plants, many of them of Mediterranean origin. The idea came to John Bond, Keeper of the Gardens, during the devastating drought year of 1976. The whole area is mulched with pea beach gravel, which is added to each year, making it drier and increasingly suitable for a large range of plants adapted to hot dry spells, which, since 1976 have become a fairly regular feature of the summers in many parts of the country. It is also a particularly good example of how the Savill Garden is used to pioneer different gardening styles.

Now the main collection of modern roses is grown in a large traditional Rose Garden surrounded by a clipped hedge.

In 1951 a great wall seventy feet long and eighteen feet high was built from bricks salvaged from London wartime bombed buildings. Facing south, with buttresses every twenty feet, it was designed specifically for a whole range of tender specimens such as *Azara dentata*, and *Fremontodendron* (*F. californicum* x *F. mexicanum*) 'California Glory'. In front of the wall are a series of raised beds planted with sun-loving alpines.

The Savill was one of the first gardens in Britain to introduce raised bed gardening, not only as an ideal environment for the plants, but to demonstrate a style of gardening which is particularly suited to elderly and disabled people.

At around this time a blaze of colour was also introduced with a collection of day lilies (hemerocallis) and bearded irises from Sandilands near Woking in Surrey, the home of Harry Randall, the first chairman of the London Electricity Board and an outstanding horticulturist, who specialised in irises and hemerocallis, as well as roses, fruit and daffodils.

One of Sir Eric Savill's ambitions for the garden was that it should contain as comprehensive a collection of plants as was possible, and this included those too tender to be trusted outside, such as the maddenii and edgworthii sections of rhododendrons. The problem was to find somewhere to grow them, and this was resolved by the use of the old lean-to greenhouse which had been used to house one of the largest vines in the country before the war, and for tomatoes during the war.

When it was demobbed it was used to house a collection of rhododendrons, including *Rh. edgworthii*, *Rh. bullatum*, *Rh. cubitii*, *Rh. nuttallii*, *Rh. valentinianum*, *Rh. megacalyx*,

utumn cascade: *Vitis coignetiae*

Rh. rhabdotum, *Rh. lindleyi*, *Rh johnstoneanum*, and Australia's only native rhododendron, *Rh. lochae*, as well as the so-called azaleas, *Rh. simsii* and *Rh. oldhamii*. Room was also found for *Jasminum polyanthum*, *Prostanthera ovalifolia*, *Lonicera hildebrandiana* and *Passiflora van volxemii*.

The old vinery served its purpose for nearly twenty years, but its size, as well as the fact that it was not designed to house temperate zone plants, restricted the expansion of the collection.

In 1963 the first purpose-built temperate house was erected. It was one hundred and twenty feet long and thirty feet wide, with a framing of western red cedar. It too did good service, but its fate was sealed by the great gales of 1987 and 1990 when it was damaged beyond repair.

April 1994 saw work start on the present one hundred and twenty by sixty feet Queen Elizabeth Temperate House. After a search for the right designer it was decided to appoint the architect Nicholas Thompson of the Cole Thompson Partnership. He and his firm had never been involved in designing a horticultural building before, but they understood the need for the building to be part of the garden rather than something quite separate.

Facing east, it is set in woodland, and is part of the woodland itself. The building was finished in June 1994, and the compost to make the beds was brought in in August and September. Planting took place over the winter, and it was opened by the Queen in April 1995. It was built by Wates Intregra. In 1996 it won the Downland Design Award for Architecture, and the commendation of the jury stated:

'Its unusual wedge shape seems to fit extremely well into the marvellous landscaped setting of these beautiful gardens. The structure is economical and the detailing of the elements well-considered.'

Rather than being a display of a collection of plants, it is a garden in its own right, with superb tree ferns (*Dicksonia antarctica*), tender rhododendrons, including the Vireya rhododendrons from south-east Asia, with their beautiful waxy tubular flowers; acacias; gardenia-scented *Michelia doltsopa*; camellias, and tropical irises such as *Iris wattii*, *I. confusa*, *I. formosana* and *I. japonica*, and superb ferns.

A gully in front of the Temperate House, fondly known as the sheep dip, has been utilised as a bedding canal. Densely planted with early colour like the bright pink *Primula* (polyanthus) 'Crescendo', it creates a surprisingly apt doorstep from the English woodland garden to an exotic sub-tropical flora.

Although they had to be contrived in the first place, the majority of the features in the garden have a completely natural look, particularly the raised peat beds, which are supported by duff, which are blocks cut out of the compressed needles and bark from the floor of conifer forests.

In 1963 the restaurant was built on a site which gives a view of plantings in which foliage and form are the most important feature. It also gives visitors enticing peeps and glimpses of what awaits them in the garden. Immediately around the perimeter of the restaurant is the raised ha-ha and bank beds of shrubs and annuals that would be ideal in any modern garden, such as *Pinus mugo* 'Carsten's Wintergold', which is at its best in the winter months. It is backed by the dwarf *Prunus incisa* 'Kojo-No-Mai', and mats of the prostrate blue *Juniperus horizontalis* 'Coast of Maine'. This is part of the deliberate policy of inspiring keen gardeners who are seeking solutions to their own planting problems.

Summer bedding is a striking feature of the curving border leading to the New Zealand Collection with bold groups of gazania, osteospermum, *Lotus berthelotii* and felicia.

The New Zealand Collection is a relative newcomer. It originated with a gift to the Queen from the government and people of New Zealand, and was inaugurated by the Queen on 23 June 1989. Originally New Zealanders had wanted to plant an avenue of their native trees in the garden, but these would not have thrived; and so a special area was created for a collection of New Zealand plants.

Set on a free-draining slope, the shrubs and herbaceous plants bring a new dimension to British gardening, particularly container gardening.

Like all great gardens, the Savill Garden does not stand still. Changes take place, some as a result of natural disasters, such as the devastating wind storm of October 1987. The storm, which reached hurricane force, destroyed the beech trees which grew on the site of the Friends' Grove, replanted by the Friends of Savill Garden with silver limes (*Tilia tomentosa*), and with blue and white crocuses naturalised in the grass. The Friends were formed from season ticket holders, and apart from raising money for projects, they also give their time to act as guides.

With the loss of the beech trees, one of the great glories of the garden disappeared. This was the so-called Moss Garden, which, in fact, was a completely natural occurrence, formed by immigrant moss, *Leucadendron argenteum*, growing into an enormous carpet of vibrant green, which would turn almost white in hot summers. It is a moss of beech woods and acid soil, but needs the cover of the trees to survive.

The storm of 1990 was not quite so destructive, but it did take out the wood, originally planted in 1780. Now it has been replanted with beech (fagus), oak (quercus) and sweet gum (liquidambar), and has been renamed the Arboretum.

As in other great gardens in the south and south-east, the 1987 storm was an horrific event. Although on the edge of its awesome progress, both the Savill Garden and the Valley Gardens were caught, and caught badly. About two thousand trees were brought crashing to the ground. All normal duties were suspended for three months while everyone turned to clearing the damage. Fortunately the loss of canopy was not so great as to seriously damage the rhododendrons, and the gaps were quickly filled in with the quite fast growing North American red oak (*Quercus rubra*), and Asian magnolias.

The Savill Garden is an enchanted place. The more you visit it, the more it reveals itself in some narrow path you overlooked, or in a piece of perfect planting. To really know it you must go back again and again, because it is never the same from one visit to the next.

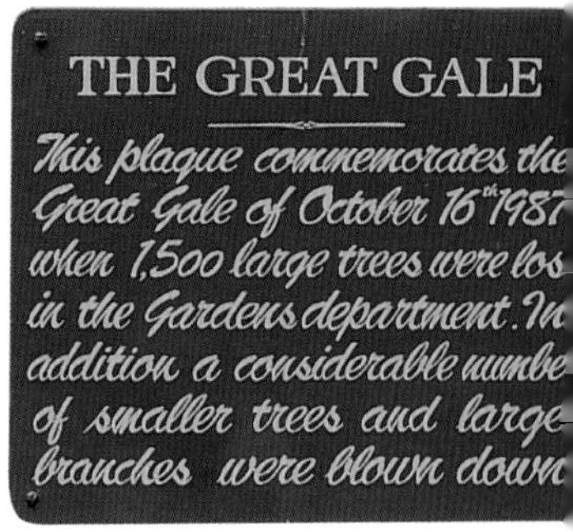
THE GREAT GALE
This plaque commemorates the
Great Gale of October 16th
when 1,500 large trees were
in the Gardens department.
addition a considerable
of smaller trees and large
branches were blown

Sad memories

Opposite: Cool Solomon's seal and hot evergreen azaleas ('Hatsugiri')

Overleaf: Azaleas by the Upper Pond

from the cavalcade of flowers that is only a few weeks away, particularly, it seems to me, the superb willow-leaf podocarp (*Podocarpus salignus*) in the centre of the wide grass walk between the herbaceous borders.

There are still some fruits on the trees and shrubs, certainly enough to attract a flock of screeching and surprising Indian ring-necked parakeets, which escaped into the wild years ago. They bring an exotic touch to the gardens, which is added to by ancient wisterias swarming sixty feet or more into oak trees like jungle lianas, or is it the tangled rigging of a foundered ship. The scrambling hydrangea (*H. petiolaris*) clambers up oaks in the garden for all the world like a tropical climbing fern. In the autumn the huge heart-shaped leaves of the crimson glory vine (*Vitis coignetiae*) coiling up a sweet chestnut above the herbaceous border will be a cloak of imperial purple.

The first touches of flower colour are to be found among the plants in the Temperate House, but even outside you can tell that the new season is on the move with the catkins on alder and birch just beginning to stretch, and leaf buds showing signs of swelling.

March is the time to come again to the garden when even the sharpest weather fails to hold back the early flowers; the clusters of snowflakes (*Leucojum vernum* var. *carpathicum*) with gold tips to the white petals; snowdrops (galanthus); sheets of blue and white crocus cultivars in the grass in the Friends' Grove. The moss on old tree stumps has taken on a bright fresh greenness.

Narcissus 'March Sunshine' is living up to its name. The hoop-petticoat daffodil (*N. bulbocodium citrinus*) is out, and there are *N. cyclamineus* everywhere, particularly growing in sheets in the lawn in front of the summerhouse, which was built in 1992 by the Friends of the Savill Garden. The first Lenten lilies (*N. pseudonarcissus*) are opening, and among the damp-loving plants there is a group of a curious greeny-yellow, very double, daffodil with finely pointed petals, called *N.* 'Rip Van Winkle'.

On the alpine beds in front of the great wall a bright red tulip (*Tulipa pulchella* 'Eastern Star') is in flower along with scillas.

Among the great plant collections grown in the Savill and Valley Gardens is that of pieris, sometimes called the lily of the valley bush because of its clusters of white, pink and red lily of the valley-like flowers, which are followed by pink, red or bronze new leaves.

Throughout the Savill Garden are magnificent groups of pieris which bring a glory to it during the spring. *P.* 'Firecrest' has masses of ivory-white flowers and bright red young growth. A cross between *P. formosa* F. 8945 x *P. japonica*, it was given an Award of Merit by the Royal Horticultural Society in 1973 for its foliage, and another in 1981 for its flowers.

Everywhere you turn there is another cultivar to be admired: *P. japonica* 'Tickled Pink'; *P. j.* 'Grayswood', whose buds are slightly bronze; *P.* 'White Pearl'; *P. yakushimanum* 'Prelude', which is yellow-green in bud; *P. japonica* 'Shojo'; *P. j.* 'Valley Rose', and one of the most widely grown of all, *P.* 'Forest Flame', which is a cross between *P. formosa* var. *forrestii* and *P. japonica*.

Camellias, too, are braving the frosts, such as the lovely white *Camellia* 'Cornish Snow' (*C. cuspidata* x *C. saluenensis*); *C.* x *vernalis* (*C. japonica* x *C. sasanqua*), with its small white, semi-double flowers, and the semi-double deep rose-pink *C. japonica* 'Gloire de Nantes'. *Cornus mas* is like golden yellow foam.

Beside the stream that flows between the Upper and Lower Pond is a kind of water meadow where damp-loving plants grow, and none are more splendid at this time of year than the brazen-yellow spathes of the so-called skunk cabbage (*Lysichiton americanus*), and the pure white spathes of *L. camtschatcensis*. The green rosettes of primulas are appearing along the stream bank.

Running virtually parallel with the stream are the raised peat beds revetted with duff blocks, and now bright with lungworts (pulmonaria), many of them with elegantly mottled leaves; very pale blue *Pulmonaria saccharata* 'Blue Mist', and deep blue *P. s.* 'Leopard'; the intense gentian-blue of *P. angustifolia* 'Azurea', and the spring-sky colour of *P. officinalis* 'Cambridge Blue'.

Daphne laureola is in bloom among the deep plum purple *Helleborus orientalis*, the heavily speckled yellows and pinks of *H. orientalis* hybrids, and the jade green flowers flushed with red-purple of *H. foetidus*.

The most delicate peat bed flowers out now are the hepaticas. *Hepatica nobilis* (*triloba*) 'Rubra Plena', with its very double deep rose-red flowers, and the white, occasionally flushed with blue, *H. nobilis* 'Alba'. Lesser celandines (*Ranunculus ficaria*) in a multitude of forms colonise spare spaces, nooks and crannies.

Elsewhere in the garden the rhododendrons are erupting with colour.

The scarlet waxy *Rh.* (*arboreum* x *haematodes*); *Rh.* 'Choremia Tower Court'; yellow *Rh. lutescens*; deep ruby red *Rh. forrestii* var. *repens* K-W. 6932 x *barbatum*; deep pink *Rh.* 'Tessa' (*moupinense* x *praecox*); the very deep pink of *Rh.* 'Pink Silk' (*cilpinense selfed*); *Rh.* x *cilpinense*, a cross made at Bodnant in Wales, between *Rh. ciliatum* and *moupinense*, which is pink in the bud and fades to white; deep pink *Rh.* 'Airy Fairy' (*lutescens* x *mucronulatum*), and the superb *Rh. sutchuenense*, which is white flushed purple-pink with a deep purple blotch in the throat.

Although the leaves are unfurled, the coral-coloured bark of *Acer palmatum* 'Sango Kaku' (syn. 'Senkaki') holds its own with the rhododendrons. The last of the golden spider flowers of witch hazel (*Hamamelis mollis*) are hanging on.

The Temperate House is flooded with the heady gardenia scent from the magnolia-like flowers of *Michelia doltsopa* 'Silver Cloud', and the white tubes of the paperbush (*Edgeworthia papyrifera*). Two fine tender rhododendrons are out – the pure white *Rh. leucaspis* from south-west China, and the pink *Rh.* (*cubitii* x *moupinense*).

With no frost to worry about in the house, the camellias are flawless such as the pitardii hybrid 'Snippet'; the white blush *C. japonica* 'Mrs. D.W. Davis'; the small tightly double pink *C. rusticana* x *lutchuensis*; deep pink *C. reticulata*, and the pink, slightly fragrant white 'Ariel's Song' (*C. fraterna* x *C. tsai*).

From Australia there are the spider flowers, *Grevillea* 'Canberra Gem' (*G. juniperinus* x *rosmarinifolia*) with iridescent pink claw-like flowers, and the magenta claws of *G. thyrsoides*. Close by is the Australian fuchsia (*Correa pulchella*) with its cherry-red pendent

Above: Lichens and mosses: a garden in miniature

Left: Fly agaric

Opposite: The Moss Garden: a great loss

tubes with a yellow mouth.

Early April and the gardens are bursting into flower everywhere you look. *Camellia* 'Cornish Snow' has been joined by the bright pink *C.* 'Inspiration' (*reticulata* x *saluenensis*), and the hugely successful and well-loved *C.* x *williamsii* 'Donation' (*saluenensis* x *japonica* 'Donckelarii') with its strong, clear pink flowers.

Two glorious magnolias, *M.* x *loebneri* 'Leonard Messel' (*kobus* x *stellata rosea*), *M.* x *loebneri* 'Merrill' (*kobus* x *stellata*), and *M. stellata* itself, are in flower. Also in flower is the silver maple (*Acer saccharinum*) which comes from eastern North America. They are green and rose coloured and appear before the leaves. People tend to think of maples in terms of autumn colour only, but now and over the coming weeks is the time to look for the delicate maple flowers.

The green-yellow flowers of *Rh. lutescens* are fully out, and so are the pale yellow trusses of 'Golden Oriole' and 'Talavera', both (*moupinense* white form x *sulfureum*).

Another two pieris are blooming. The red *P. japonica* 'Valley Valentine' and *P. japonica* 'Pink Delight'. By the stone bridge is a little clump of butcher's broom (*Ruscus aculeatus*) displaying tiny flowers in the centre of the leaves. If you look at them through a hand lens they are quite exotic – plum purple set in a nest of green. In the autumn the leaves will have bright red berries like rubies in the centre.

In the damp areas the lysichitons are still displaying their yellow and white banners, and there are pools of golden kingcups or marsh marigolds (*Caltha palustris*), and clumps of the beautiful blue parasitical plant, toothwort (*Lathraea clandestina*). Mauve pasque flowers (*Pulsatilla halleri*), and the fresh white form *P. vulgaris* 'Alba'; lavender-pink *Primula vulgaris* ssp. *sibthorpii*, white *Ranunculus ficaria*, and the orange *R. f.* 'Cupreus', shooting stars (dodecatheon) and the windflowers (*Anemone nemorosa*) light up the ground under the trees and shrubs.

Two fine forms of the Algerian iris (*I. unguicularis*), the dark blue 'Mary Barnard', and the pale blue 'Walter Butt' are in full bloom on the raised beds below the wall, together with *Tulipa neustruevae*, with its starry golden yellow flowers with a green stripe down the midrib, the pink flowers of *Arctostaphylos canescens* from California, and on the wall *Trachelospermum jasminoides* 'Variegatum', with its pink, green and cream leaves. The summer blooming flowers are sweetly fragrant.

By the middle of the month *Rh.* 'Beatrice Keir' (*lacteum* x 'Logan Damaris'), which is bright yellow in bud, but paler when the corollas open, and the unusual blue-pink *Rh.* 'P.J. Mezzit' (*carolinianum* x *dauricum*), which was awarded an Award of Merit in 1972, have joined the other rhododendrons.

In the sloping bed in front of the Temperate House the young growth of *Euphorbia dulcis* 'Chameleon' is a rich plum purple, while in the house itself there is a great mass of flower.

The orchid-like soft blue flowers of *Iris japonica* and *I. j.* 'Variegata' are studding the arching stems; *Oxalis hedysaroides* from Central America is a mass of yellow; *Michelia doltsopa* 'Silver Cloud' and *M. maudiae* L/S. 1081–83 from eastern China are flooding the building with their heady scent. From southern China is *Dichroa versicolor* with huge purple-tinged leaves and dense heads of mauve-blue flowers.

Safe from the uncertain spring weather, the trusses on the rhododendrons are impec-

Colchicum 'Conquest', whose early autumn flowers brighte[n] the woodland garden

Cornus 'Ormonde'

Opposite: A scene in the Bog Garden

h. 'Choremia Tower Court'

cable. *Rh. bullatum* x *moupinense* has white flowers and soft, furry leaves. Those of *Rh.* 'Candy' look like tropical jasmine; *Rh. cubitii* 'Ashcombe', First Class Certificate 1962, is apple-blossom pink with an orange throat; *Rh. edgworthii* x *ciliatum*, white flushed pink, and in contrast to these soft colours, *Rh. burmanicum* 'Elizabeth David' is bright sulphur yellow.

The camellias are also magnificent, and in some cases the flowers are almost unbelievably large, such as the huge red ones of *C.* 'Dr. Clifford Parks' (*reticulata* 'Crimson Robe' x *japonica* 'Kramer's Surprise'). *C.* 'Nicky Crisp' (*pitardii* x *japonica*) is a soft pink, *C. reticulata* 'Captain Rawes', vermillion, and *C. rusticana* x *lutchuensis*, with its tightly double pink flowers has a delightful weeping habit.

May is the month when the spring gathers together everything, cast, chorus, orchestra, the whole company, to put on the greatest show of the season.

Ethel Armitage, who wrote an enchanting book, *A Country Garden*, recalled taking a schoolboy into her orchard to enjoy the beauties of the day.

'. . . I suppose, I became rather lyrical about it, and he, in consequence, extremely bored. For when we had reached the top and were looking down on the pink and white of apple blossom and the tender green of young leaf, he turned to me and said: "Oh, I see you are like Ovid, mad on spring."'

Well, like Ovid, I am mad on spring, and in particular May in the Savill Garden.

You are greeted with the foaming pink blossom of the Japanese cherry, *Prunus incisa* 'Oshidori', and the white heather bells of the Californian *Arctostaphylos pumila. Viola labradorica* is a mass of deep blue flowers standing out from the purple leaves.

On the slope down to the ponds the mauve-pink of *Bergenia purpurascens* var. *delavayi*, and the dark pink of *B.* 'Admiral' are a rich contrast to the fresh green of new leaves and catkins of silver birch (*Betula pendula*). The pink-tipped white bracts of *Cornus* 'Ormonde' (*nuttalli* x *florida*) are fully open.

There are still masses of kingcups, but the flowers of *Pieris* 'Forest Flame' have given way to the bright red cockades of new leaves. The tufts of white flowers, which are tinged with green in the bud, are coming out on *Fothergilla major*. Acers are unfolding their delicate spring foliage. They are green and gold on *Acer negundo* 'Kelly's Gold', with long silky strands of flowers dangling beneath them.

Hosta and colchicum leaves are appearing among the shrubs, and the tightly coiled fronds of ferns are just breaking through the soil. White and purple snake's head fritillaries (*Fritillaria meleagris*) are in flower, and so are the mauve and white drumstick primulas (*Primula denticulata*). The yellow strawberry flowers and shiny green leaves of *Waldsteinia ternata* from Japan and China, and the giant Pyrennean buttercup (*Ranunculus gouanii*), put on a fine show.

In the herbaceous borders the gardeners are staking the plants with pea sticks and boughs, mainly birch, woven together for the summer spectacular which will start in June and July, and last until the autumn. When the plants are fully grown there will be no sign of the supports that make them grow so strong and tall.

The weeping silver pear (*Pyrus salicifolia* 'Pendula') is spangled with white blossom, while our magnificent native cherry, the gean, the double form, (*Prunus avium* 'Plena') is one great mass of pure white double flowers. In almost startling contrast close by is

Above: Gentiana acaulis

Left: Wisteria sinensis

Opposite top: Rh. burmanicum enlivens the Temperate House

Opposite bottom: Trillium grandiflorum 'Flore Pleno'

Raised beds in autumn

Walking is a slow business for rhododendron lovers in the garden at this time of the year when you can't help stopping to admire the lavender-pink *Rh. concinnum* x *pseudochrysanthum*; the yellow *Rh. campylocarpum* x (*wardii* x *calophytum*); the waxy ox-blood red *Rh.* ('Kiev' x 'Gipsy King'), and the pink of 'Blewberry' (*roxieanum* x *anhweiense*).

Rh. 'Cornish Cross' (*griffithianum* x *thomsonii*) not only has particularly lovely flowers which are cherry-red in the bud opening to pale pink, but it also has the most wonderful flaky grey-mauve bark.

Also to catch the eye are the bright red flowers of *Rh.* 'Elizabeth' (*forrestii* var. *repens* x *griersonianum*), the pink bells of 'Veryan Bay' (*pseudochrysanthum* x *williamsianum*), the deeper pink of 'Temple Bell' (*orbiculare* x *williamsianum*), and the pert plum-coloured bells of the Himalayan dwarf, *Rh. pumilum*.

In the Temperate House three fine rhododendrons are out; the intense red tubes of *Rh.* 'Saint Valentine' (*lochiae* x *gracilentum*), the yellow gold of *Rh.* 'Flamenco', and the creamy-white *Rh. johnstoneanum*.

Two magnolias are displaying their noble colours; the rich purple *M.* 'Randy' (*liliiflora* 'Nigra' x *stellata*), and the softer purple flush of *M.* 'Betty' (*liliiflora* 'Nigra' x *stellata* 'Rosea').

Under a group of rhododendrons the huge, shiny green leaves of the giant Himalayan lily (*Cardiocrinum giganteum*) have unfolded. In a few weeks there will be sturdy stems, five or six feet tall, bearing magnificent white scented trumpets. Spanish bluebells (*Hyacinthoides hispanica* 'Chevithorne') are almost in flower.

In this part of the garden, just above Home Wood Lawn, is a beautiful piece of planting – the dusky pink of *Camellia* x *williamsii* 'Donation', and the blue of *Rh. augustinii* x *rubiginosum*.

There is a little grove of snowy mesipilus (*Amelanchier lamarckii*) from North America smothered with white blossom and underplanted with *Hosta undulata* var. *univittata*, and an American fern, *Onoclea sensibilis*.

What makes this such a special time in the garden is the contrast between the strong colours of some of the rhododendrons and the delicacy of the pink strings of blossom on the cherry, *Prunus padus* 'Colorata', the pale green film of new needles on the larch trees and the green gold of sycamore leaves (*Acer pseudoplatanus*).

Glaucidium palmatum, which is a member of the paeonia family, and comes from Japan, has opened its mauve-blue flowers. To me they look like little abutilon flowers, but others see them closer to paeonias themselves. The bells of *Mertensia virginica* are sky blue, and a wonderful contrast to the coral-pink new growth of *Pieris* 'Bert Chandler'.

Throughout the garden the fronds of the noble royal fern (*Osmunda regalis*) are stretching upwards. The bellwort (*Uvularia perfoliata*) has yellow-green clematis-like flowers. There are sheets of the rose-pink *Primula rosea*, along with *P. sieboldii* 'Deechin', which is pale blue with frilly edges to the petals.

White wake robin (*Trillium grandiflorum*), and its dark purple cousin *Trillium erectum*, grow among a sea of dog's-tooth violets (*Erythronium revolutum*) and *E.* 'White Beauty'. With a promise of lushness to come the leaves of rodgersia and *Gunnera manicata* are

Meconopsis x *sheldonii*

Opposite: Summer contrasts

eranium maderense

pposite and this page right top nd bottom: The Temperate Iouse: a botanical treasury

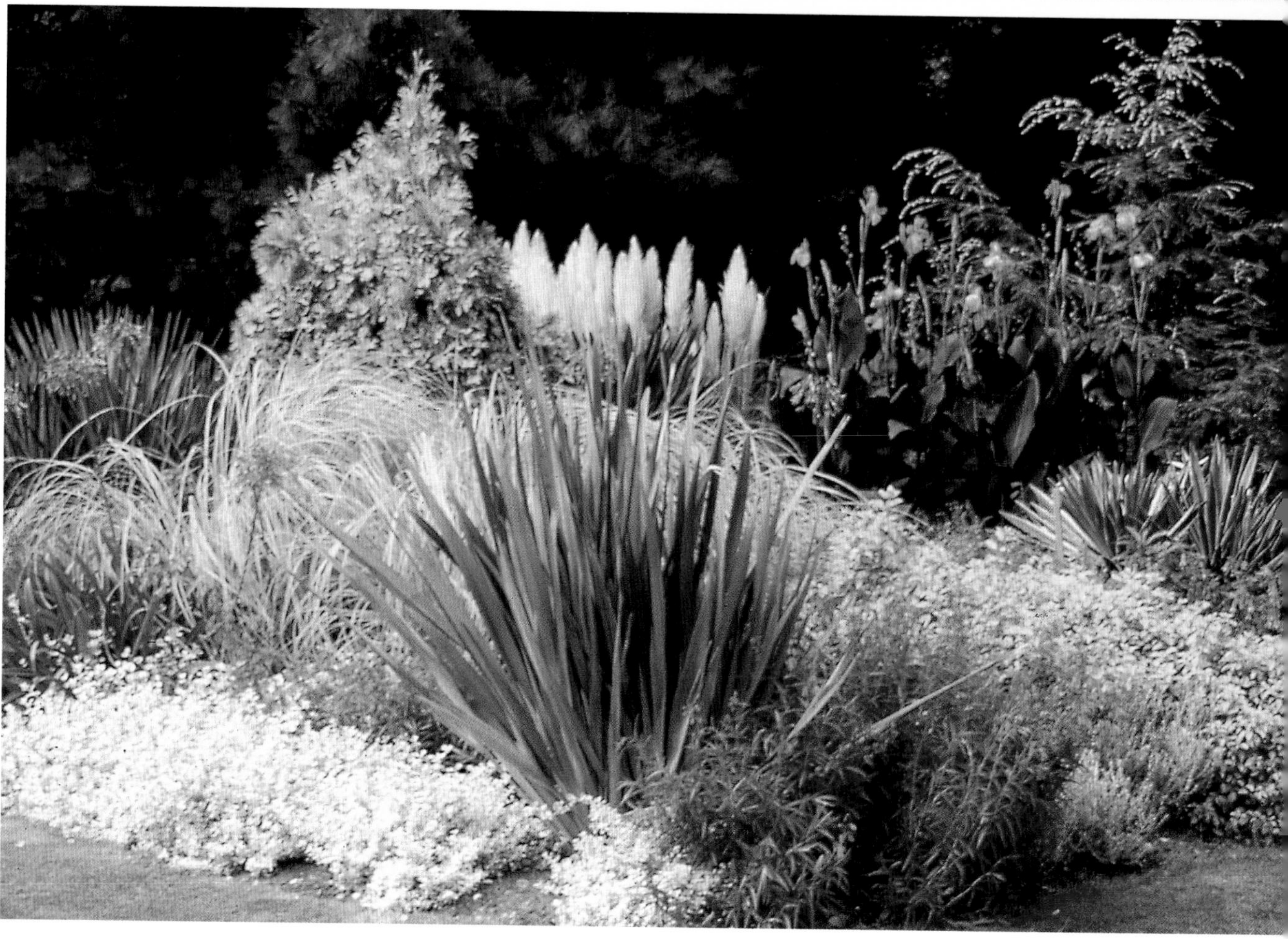

, left and right: High summer

tom: Diversity of form and
our: an island bed

Outside the Temperate House the herbaceous borders are coming to life with the striking foliage of the plume poppy (*Macleaya microcarpa*), and the giant seakale (*Crambe cordifolia*). In the nearby Dry Garden, *Euphorbia characias* ssp. *wulfenii* is bright with golden-lime bracts, in contrast to the cool white spikes of *Asphodelus asiaticus*.

After a mid-May trip you are left with one enduring memory, which is another example of perfect planting – the shrimp-pink young leaves of *Acer palmatum* 'Brilliantissima' among red *Camellia japonica* 'Rubescens Major', and pink cherry blossom.

On the last day of May the warmth of early summer has soaked into the garden. The carp in the Upper and Lower Ponds are feeding on the surface with lip-smacking contentment, and the azaleas are still out on the banks of the Upper Pond. The leaves of the skunk cabbage are huge now, and the bright yellow and white of their spathes has been replaced by the blue of *Iris sibirica*. The flower buds on the neat-leaved *Viburnum atrocyaneum* are breaking. Banks of *Rh. luteum* are filling the air with the richest fragrance from their golden flowers, and not far from them *Rh.* 'Mayday' (*griersonianum* x *haematodes*) is brilliant scarlet, but not dominating the peachy-yellow of *Rh.* 'Golden Torch' ('Bambi' x 'Grosclaude' x *griersonianum*), given an Award of Merit in 1984, and the glowing rose pink of the large cup-shaped corollas of *Rh.* 'Vintage Rose' (*yakushimanum* x 'Jalisco Eclipse' x 'Fusilier'). A magnolia of great beauty with purple flowers stained with ochre is in full glory. It is *M.* x *brooklynensis* 'Ava Maria' (*acuminata* x *liliiflora*). Among the underplanting is one of the most graceful of all ferns, with its fine leaves and wiry black stems, *Adiantum pedatum*, a native of North America and Japan.

Yellow *Iris innominata* from the Pacific coast of America is blooming on the raised beds in the wall garden, along with the curious three-petalled white flowers of *Libertia formosa*. On the wall is the double yellow form of *Rosa banksiae* and the pale pink *R.* x *anemonoides* (*laevigata* x *R.* x *odorata*), and the pretty cousin of the kiwi fruit, *Actinidia kolomikta*, with its green, white and pink leaves.

Walk on from the wall and you are back amongst the rhododendrons and shrubs, as well as the sweetly scented *Primula prolifera* (syn. *helodoxa*), and the deep red *P. pulverulenta*. The leaves of *Hosta* 'Blue Wedgewood' are startlingly blue. *Rh.* 'Charlotte de Rothschild' (*discolor* x 'St. Keverne') has huge pink flowers.

Cornus florida is looking superb, and so is *Cornus alternifolia* 'Argentea' with its layered cream and green leaves.

But truly outstanding is *Wisteria floribunda* 'Macrobotrys' climbing sixty feet up an oak tree with flowers cascading down like blue icicles.

Two unusual trees now in full young leaf are the variegated tulip tree (*Liriodendron tulipifera*), planted by Queen Elizabeth, the Queen Mother, in 1982 to mark the fiftieth anniversary of the garden, and the golden oak (*Quercus rubra* 'Aurea').

By the middle of June the Savill Garden has become transformed by the summer blooms. The green of the leaves of the trees and shrubs has deepened, while the flowers of the bedding plants are hot and sunny. The bright orange of *Gazania splendens* and its cultivars like the pale purple 'Christopher', bright yellow 'Michael', pink and white 'Dazzler', and the mauve-pink of *Osteospermum barberiae* create a tropical look.

Lotus berthelotii, with its filigree silver-grey foliage has been bedded out and will soon be covered with orange-red parrot beak flowers.

Those of *Felicia amelloides* 'Santa Anita' seem to reflect the sky, and so does *Ceanothus* 'Blue Mound'.

There are softer colours in the layers of white petals of *Viburnum tomentosum* 'Nanum Semperflorens', *Potentilla fruticosa* 'Princess', a cotoneaster species from south China GU1Z. 128, tumbling over a wall, and covered with butterflies and bees. Pink cistus, and the ruby red trumpets and gold leaves of *Weigela florida* 'Rubrigold' put on a brave show, but there is one corner of the gardens which is outstanding now; it is the New Zealand Garden.

The collection of New Zealand plants is housed partly in a cold greenhouse, but principally on a bankside site. Those plants that need protection are grown in large pots so that they can be brought under cover for the winter.

An information exhibition is in a separate small building, and this should be the first port of call. Coming out of it there is a group of containers planted with the sculptural golden *Astelia fragrans*, the gleaming *Astelia chathamica* 'Silver Sword', *Phormium cookianum*, the marvellous red, cream, green and pale gold *P.* 'Rainbow Queen', and cordylines.

Like anywhere else in the Savill Garden, the New Zealand Collection is a learning experience for keen gardeners, particularly those who are confined to a patio, terrace or small courtyard, for here are plants ideally suited for this style of gardening, particularly the leptospermums, with their tiny, neat leaves and flowers that encrust the twigs like bright barnacles.

Leptospermum scoparium has produced some superb cultivars, especially the shades of pink to be found in 'Blossom', 'Charmer', 'Coral Candy', 'Nanum Tui', 'Pink Cascade', 'Gaiety Girl' and 'Keatley'. There are also deep velvety reds like 'Red Damask', 'Roland Boyce' and 'Burgundy Queen', as well as the virginal whites of 'Leonard Wilson' and 'Snow Flurry'.

New Zealand plants have a unique charm like the hebes, particularly *H. macrantha* with its large white flowers, and gems like the low growing *Sophora prostrata* 'Little Baby' covered with what look like small orange birds bills, and *Parrahebe cataractae*, with its bright blue speedwell blooms.

There can scarcely be a more delightful ground-cover plant than *Acaena novae-zelandiae* whose flowers become bronze-purple burrs. Outstanding in the collection is *Acaena* 'Blue Haze' with blue leaves and bronze buds on long bronze-purple stems.

The New Zealand laurel (*Griselinia littoralis*) has thick apple-green leaves which set off the other plants in the collection, and include the lovely cream and green variegated variety 'Dixon's Cream'. The same is true of the holly-like leaves of *Olearia macrodonta*, which later in the summer will be smothered with clusters of white daisy flowers. *O. insignis*, also known as *Pachystegia insignis*, opens its daisy flowers earlier.

Another striking shrub is the lancewood (*Pseudopanax lessonii* 'Purpureum'), with its bronze-purple foliage. Bronze foliage is very characteristic of New Zealand plants, particularly the sedge (*Carex plagellifera*), which looks so good close to the pure white flowers of *Linum monogynum*, or the tiny white daisy flowers held on long fine stalks of

Mahonia x *media* 'Charity'

the rare langenophoxa. Daisy flowers are also very typical of New Zealand plants, and are probably at their best on the mountain daisy (celmisia). *Celmisia longifolia*, which is grown in the cool house, is outstanding with its gleaming silver leaves and white flowers with the petals slightly turned down. Another delight in the house is the bronze form of *Anthropodium candidum*, with its grassy leaves and minute white flowers.

For grace little can compare with *Carmichaelia robusta* and *C. aligera*, whose slender branches are covered with pale lavender flowers.

Leaving the collection you can make your way down to the stream. The scent of *Rh. luteum* is heady, and there are rhododendrons still in flower, like the almost prostrate bright red *Rh.* 'Joseph Hill' (*nakaharae* x 'W. Leith'). The superb white bracts of *Cornus kousa*, and the pink ones of *C. k.* 'Satomi' are fully open, as are the clusters of white flowers of *Viburnum atrocyaneum*.

But it is the ferns which are quite superb at this time of the year. The fronds have uncoiled and they are in their early summer colours.

The lady fern (*Athyrium filix-femina* 'Fieldii'), and the dwarf form, *A. f-f.* 'Minutissimum'; the five-fingered maidenhair fern (*Adiantum pedatum*) with its black stalks and pale green swallow-wing leaves, and the really tiny form *A. p.* var. *subpumilum*; the broad buckler fern (*Dryopteris dilatata*); the cinnamon fern (*Osmunda cinnamonea*), which is smaller than its noble cousin, the regal fern (*O. regalis*), which is to be found in huge and magnificent colonies wherever there is a damp spot in the garden; the soft-shield fern (*Polystichum setiferum* 'Plumosum Bevis'), and the slender creeping Australian hard fern (*Blechnum penna-marina*).

In the Temperate House the bird of paradise (*Strelitzia reginae*) is in flower and looking exactly like the head of some fantastic bird. It is easy to imagine the fascination and amazement it must have caused when it was introduced from South Africa by Francis Masson in the eighteenth century. It was the first plant that Sir Joseph Banks wrote down in his list of three hundred plants that King George III sent to Empress Catherine II of Russia in 1795. It was named in honour of Queen Charlotte, who had such an influence on the gardens of Frogmore. Before her marriage to the king she had been Charlotte of Mecklenburg-Strelitz.

Geranium maderense and *Iris wattii* are still in flower, joined by the towering tangerine spikes of *Watsonia meriana*. Peering out from among its clover leaves are the pure blue pea flowers of *Parochetus africanus*. Two rhododendrons, the gorgeous gold *Rh.* 'Flamenco Dancer' (*aurigeranum* x *maccregoriae*), and the deep pink evergreen azalea *Rh.* 'Salmon's Leap', with pretty variegated foliage.

The great double herbaceous border – each two hundred feet long by thirty-four feet wide – are giving tantalising hints of what is to come with the ruby flowers of *Geranium psilostemon*; *Penstemon* 'Drinkstone Ruby'; the flawless white *Cosmos bipinnatus* 'Purity'; *Dictamnus albus* 'Purpureus', and *D. albus*; the blue tinged white flowers of *Tradescantia virginiana* 'Iris Pritchard', and the misty purple haze of *Thalictrum aquilegifolium* 'Thundercloud'. *Rosa* 'Nevada' is in bloom, and the heavy scent of the pink *Syringa* x *prestoniae* 'Virgilia' sweeps over the borders.

Every year the plants in one of the four huge beds of the herbaceous border are lifted and split up, and the soil double dug and manured before replanting. Next to the

idsummer glory

'he Rose Garden

verleaf: High summer

Rose Garden swags of climbing roses on ropes are beginning to flower, and in front of them the long bed has been planted for the summer with *Argyranthemum frutescens* 'Snowflake' and blue, purple and cherry red *Penstemon* 'Colegraves New Hybrids'. The annuals for this bed tend to change from year to year.

The great wall is full of colour with *Rosa* x *anemonoides* still in full flush, but now joined by the pink *Rosa* 'Climbing Cécile Brunner', and the golden cups of *Fremontodendron* 'California Glory'. The vanilla-scented *Azara serrata* from Chile is a mass of yellow flowers like tiny shaving brushes, and white *Rhaphiolepis umbellata* from south-east Asia fill the air with fragrance, while the leaves of the Australian mint bush, *Prostanthera cuneata*, give off a sweet mint aroma when they are squeezed.

Under the rhododendrons at the top of the garden the red flowers of *Meconopsis napaulensis* and *M. regia* glow like rubies, while in the shade of an oak tree a pool of azure is created by a group of the Himalayan blue poppy (*Meconopsis betonicifolia*).

American Pacific coast irises, cistus, cherry-red scorpion senna (*Coronilla emerus*) from south-east Europe, cammasia, and the glowing red *Paeonia lobata* 'Sunshine' cover the dry garden with colonies of colour.

Down by the stream and Upper and Lower Ponds the gunnera are gigantic, and on the peat beds the magnificent purple Mediterranean orchid (*Dactylorhiza elata*), and the paler form from Algeria are at their peak. So is the strange cobra-headed *Arisaema serratum* (syn. *japonicum*).

Yellow flags (*Iris pseudacorus*), the American blue flag (*I. versicolor*), and *I. sibirica* 'White Swirl' are flowering near the water. There are huge regal ferns, and under the oak trees, pernettya, now gaultheria, are out.

Towards the stone bridge there is a great clump of bamboo, which with its new leaves looks like giant ostrich plumes. The climbing hydrangea on the oak is beginning to flower. Bowles golden wood grass (*Milium effusum* 'Aureum') lights up the undergrowth, and the calico bush (*Kalmia latifolia*) is coming into bloom among the rhododendrons.

With the passing of the exuberance of spring, thick carpets of fallen corollas under the rhododendron trees and bushes are a fleeting reminder of what has gone before, and the pace in the Savill Garden slows to match the lazy days of summer. The bright sunny flowers of helianthemums, so perfectly named sun roses, tumble over the walls of the ha-ha by the restaurant. Lilies are flowering among the shrubs, competing as best they can with the grandeur of their close cousin, the giant Himalayan lily (*Cardiocrinum giganteum*) with its enormous, richly scented white trumpets, striped with reddish purple on the inside.

But the great and glorious carnival of the summer garden is the magnificent herbaceous borders that sweep up to the floribunda roses before you come to the rhododendron, camellia and magnolia plantations around Home Wood Lawn.

Earlier in the year the borders had looked quite peculiar with their beehives of birch twigs woven over the plants. But now the plants have grown through the twiggy supports and are a mass of flowers and foliage. The carnival starts in quite a subdued manner, but by August and September the hot colours of annuals, like *Antirrhinum* 'Scarlet Giant', the annual carnation (*Dianthus* 'Scarlet Charm'), *Dahlia* 'Moonfire',

with its dark purple leaves and flame red flowers, and the spider flower (*Cleome spinosa* 'Violet Queen'), stitched in among perennials such as *Achillea filipendulina* 'Gold Plate', golden rod (*Solidago* 'Goldenmosa'), that most unlikely of all lettuce (*Lactuca bourgaei*), with its smoky blue flowers, the pale mauve of *Eupatorium purpureum*, the fluffy white spikes of *Cimicifuga racemosa* 'Atropurpurea', the golden brightness of x *Solidaster luteus* 'Lemore', the red leaves and pink flowers of *Heuchera* 'Rachel', and the blue-white flowers of *Penstemon* 'Mother of Pearl' combine to create a kind of medieval tapestry rolled out down a gentle slope.

Cotinus coggygria

During the late summer and early autumn *Anemone hupehensis japonica* comes into its own in the borders. There is a very fine double pink form close to the Temperate House, which combines so well with the deep pink *Polygonum amplexicaule* 'Firetail'. There is a purity about the white *Anemone* x *hybrida* 'Géantes des Blanches', and the dark pink *Anemone* x *hybrida* 'Hadspen Abundance' (*japonica* x *vitifolia*).

One of the loveliest combinations of annual and perennial is the deep purple-blue of *Heliotropium arborescens* 'Marine' with golden rod (solidago).

Because they are so large and deep, these wonderful borders can contain giants, like the almost tree-like seakale (*Crambe cordifolia*), the towering golden *Helianthus atrorubens*, and *Helianthus salicifolius*, with its smaller yellow flowers and graceful, cascading narrow willow leaves.

Superb grasses like *Molinia altissima* 'Winspiel', which grows to eight feet tall, and by catching every breath of wind brings movement to the beds, as does the cream and green barred *Miscanthus sinensis* 'Zebrinus', and *M. sinensis* 'Variegatus'.

Shades of blue are provided by the herbaceous clematis, like *C. heracleifolia* 'Wyevale', with the much richer colour of *Aster amellus* 'Nocturne', and *Agapanthus* (Headbourne Worthy hybrid) 'Royal Blue'.

More subtle colours are to be found in the grey foliage and grey-white flowers of *Lysimachia ephemerum*, and a well-behaved rose bay willow herb (*Epilobium dodonaei*).

Herbaceous borders are practically a synonym for English gardening, and one plant in particular seems to symbolise them. It is the phlox with its abundance of flowers and delicious scent. There are some lovely cultivars in the borders; *Phlox paniculata* 'Mount Fujiyama', *P. p.* 'Mother of Pearl', the pink *P. p.* 'Balmoral', and the blue-purple *P. p.* 'Hampton Court'.

Away to the right of the herbaceous borders the hybrid tea roses put on a voluptuous show; apricot-pink 'Queen Charlotte', flame-orange and pink 'Dekorat', pure white 'Pristine', clear red 'National Trust', bright red 'Precious Platinum', and velvet red 'Deep Secret', apricot 'Just Joey', pink 'Blessings', and the rich yellow 'Valencia'. In one quite narrow bed the roses are beautifully shown off by white *Hibiscus syriacus* 'Totus Albus'.

In the lawn above the Rose Garden there is more vivid colour, no more so than in a round bed where a cherry (*Prunus* 'Shirofugen') is surrounded by a bright medley of *Gazania* 'Daybreak'.

One of the most exotic beds, also close by, is planted with the orange *Dahlia* 'Forncett Furnace', the orange-gold *D.* 'David Howard', and the delicate hardy species, *D. merckii*, whose single flowers range from a pale pink, which is almost white to purple; orange,

peach and yellow canna, pink-flushed *Argyranthemum frutescens*, *Agapanthus* (Headbourne hybrid) 'Glamis Castle', the superb blues of *Salvia patens* 'Cambridge Blue', and *S. uliginosa*, are a perfect combination with the golden pampas grass (*Cortaderia selloana* 'Gold Band'), yuccas and phormium. The tropical bed was planted forty years ago, long before the style became trendy.

Equally striking is the monocot border, with ivory white summer hyacinth (*Galtonia candicans*), red hot pokers, (*Kniphofia uvaria 'Maxima'*, *K.* x *erecta*, and the fine leaved yellow *K.* 'Brimstone'), *Crocosmia* 'Lucifer', and big clumps of agapanthus.

The Dry Garden also comes into its own at this time of the year where blue willow gentian (*Gentiana asclepiadea*) is to be found close to the peach coloured *Kniphofia caulescens*. There are angel's fishing rods (*Dierama pulcherrimum*); purple pea flowers of *Indigofera potaninii*, and the jade-green seed heads of *Bupleurum fruticosum*, white *Gaura lindheimeri*, and the purple flowers the Siberian grass, *Melica altissima* 'Atropurpurea'.

Hydrangeas are to be found all over the garden; the pale blue *Hydrangea macrophylla* 'Grant's Choice', blue and pink *H. m.* 'Hamburg', and the cone shaped flower heads of *H. paniculata*, of which *H. p.* 'Tardiva', which was awarded a First Class Certificate in 1968, and *H.p.* 'Kyushu' are outstanding.

Pink and white *Cyclamen hederifolium* create tiny drifts on the peat beds, and the truncheons of orange berries of a fine form of *Arum maculatum* stand out.

By the bridge at the bottom of the Upper Pond there are clumps of *Zantedeschia aethiopica* 'Crowborough', and a pretty impatiens with small orange flowers, while the fertile pinnae of the royal fern (*Osmunda regalis*) are a rich rusty orange.

In the New Zealand Collection the burrs of the *Acaena* 'Copper Carpet' really are the colour of copper, and contrast beautifully with the fluffy beige seed heads of *Pachystegia insignis*. *Linum monogynum* is still producing flawless white flowers.

Alongside the path to the Temperate House, *Colchicum byzantinum* from Transylvania has opened its large pale violet chalices. *C.* 'William Dykes' is out, and also the pale purple *C.* 'Dandaels', and a rich, deep purple unnamed variety, which was a gift to the gardens.

Cyclamen hederifolium 'Alba' nestles in the shallow soil between two projecting roots of a hollow oak. The fronds of *Dryopteris erythrosora* from Japan and China are green and pink-bronze.

Yellow monkey musk (*Mimulus luteus*) are in cheerful disarray by the stream among deep velvety-red *Lobelia* x *speciosa* 'Dark Crusader'. There are the yellow bell flowers of one of the most elegant of all plants, *Kirengeshoma palmata*; deep purple spikes of *Astilbe chinensis* 'Pumila', and stout yellow columns of a sturdy ligularia species CLD. 1147.

The Temperate House as always is a joy. There is a brilliant parade of cannas in the sheep dip bed in front of the house, and inside the white flowers of the giant *Impatiens tinctoria*, the pale lemon yellow ones of *I. scabrida*, and the deep pink of *I. pseudoviola*, are in quiet contrast to the brightness of *Abutilon* x *hybridum* 'Red Belle', and the hot orange of the ginger lily (*Hedychium coccineum* 'Tara' SCHL. 1184) from Nepal.

There is a carnival spirit about the bunches of scarlet tubes of *Fuchsia corymbiflora* from Peru. There are still masses of yellow flowers on *Oxalis hedysaroides*, which has

anna 'Black Knight'

pposite: "Help, call in the tree rgeons!"

verleaf: Amongst the Kurume aleas in the Punch Bowl

been flowering for months. Close by the white trumpets of *Brugmansia* x *candida* give off a narcotic scent.

It is easy to spend your time in this wonderful covered garden looking up at exuberant plants, but you should also look down and discover the pretty pink *Tulbaghia capensis*, and a rich golden-yellow prostrate bedstraw from southern China, (*Lysimachia henryi*). *Rh.* 'St. Valentine' (*lochae* x *gracilentum*) is in full bright red flower, perhaps it has got in a muddle with its calendar.

Two begonias from Malaysia are quite superb now – *B. grandis* ssp. *evansiana* and *B. g.* ssp. *e.* 'Alba' – and the back wall has been made glamorous with the deep rose pink flowers of *Lapageria rosea* G. & K. 4083, which comes from Chile and Argentina.

There are massive clumps of the blue African lily (agapanthus), the soft pink bells of *Campanula vidalii*, and the somewhat funereal purple of *Rhodochiton atrosanguineum*, all of which manages to work perfectly with the blue flowers of *Dichroa versicolor* and the white flowers of an enchanting eucryphia from south Australia (*E. moorei*).

THE VALLEY GARDENS

Azalea fiesta

The Valley Gardens, which cover four hundred acres south of Smith's Lawn down to the shores of Virginia Water, are a true forest garden where great trees protect a huge collection of shrubs. Beech, birch, sweet chestnut, oak and alder, the valleys, ridgeways and narrow winding paths create a setting which is always beautiful whether in the depth of winter or vibrant with spring bloom.

Although he was writing more than one hundred years before the decision to create the Valley Gardens was taken, John Claudius Loudon could have been describing the forest trees and shrubs in the gardens in the introduction to his great work *Arboretum et Fruticum Britannicum*. He wrote: 'Everyone feels that trees are among the grandest and most ornamental objects of natural scenery: what would landscape be without them: where would be the charm of hills, plains, valleys, rocks, rivers, cascades, lakes, or islands, without the hanging wood, the widely extended forest, the open grove, the scattered groups, the varied clothing, the shape and intricacy, the contrast, and the variety of form and colour, conferred by trees and shrubs?'

He continued: 'The characteristic beauties of the general forms of trees are as various as their species; and equally so are the beauty and varieties of the ramifications of their branches, spray, buds, leaves, flowers, and fruit. The changes in the colour of the foliage of trees, at different seasons of the year, alone form a source of ever-varying beauty, and of perpetual enjoyment to the lovers of nature.'

All of this can be recognised in the Valley Gardens today.

In 1949 it was realised that there was no further scope for major expansion in the Savill Garden, and that there was no room for the thousands of plants which had been propagated in the nursery.

With the enthusiastic backing of King George VI, Sir Eric looked for a location for a second garden development. He did not have to look far. South of Smith's Lawn was an area of abandoned sandpits, which would eventually become the Heather Garden. Although it is full of dips and pits and huge potholes it is a kind of plateau which ends on the north edge of a deep wide valley, beyond which is another valley. They already had fine forest trees growing in them, and natural shelter which would be needed if exotic, and in some cases tender, shrubs and trees were to prosper. The king was convinced that it was the ideal location for the large-leaved Himalayan rhododendrons, as well as magnolias from both Asia and North America.

Most of the fine mature trees, and a number of conifers, were left to provide the structure of the garden as well as the canopy needed for the shrubs, but, like the Savill Garden at the beginning, all the rest was a tangle of undergrowth and a vast mat of bracken, which had to be cleared before any planting could begin.

Bulldozers were used to smooth off the slopes and create grassy glades, and paths made, which if you follow them take you to every part of the gardens, and which are also linked by flights of steps revetted with logs. A large water main laid under Smith's

Lawn to serve the army camp which had occupied it, was linked to an irrigation system for the gardens, whose soil is very sandy and free-draining.

By the autumn of 1950 enough land had been cleared and prepared for planting to begin. The design and layout of the gardens had been agreed, and at every stage the king and queen had been closely involved. Throughout the preparation process they had regularly visited the site, and a great many of their ideas and suggestions were put into practice.

While at this stage it was firmly established that rhododendrons, and what were then separately accepted as azaleas, would provide the dominant planting, it was decided that they should share the gardens with a wide range of trees and shrubs so that there would always be variety and interest.

A small winter garden west of the Azalea Valley was planted with winter-flowering shrubs so that it could be guaranteed that there would be something in bloom on Christmas Day.

Despite having to produce a garden which would attract visitors the year round, Sir Eric Savill wanted to retain the feel and look of a natural forest. He wanted the paths to follow the natural contours of the terrain, and to achieve this he would instruct a gardener to make his way from one point to another taking the most comfortable route, which resulted in paths that wind through the trees and shrubs, easy to walk for the pioneer and subsequently for visitors.

Except in the case of single specimens, all shrubs and trees were planted in groups of odd numbers – three, five or seven – which very easily creates a quite natural look, rather than even numbers which tend to give plantings a rigid, regimented appearance.

With the imperative being for the natural look, existing forest trees were not corralled in a circle of shrubs. Drifts of plants were set so that they seemed to encroach upon the trees and then spread out to merge with the rest of the undergrowth. This is very much as plants would grow in a natural forest or woodland situation.

Form and foliage was also a major consideration when choosing plants. A great deal of thought was given to the grouping of colours, particularly with the rhododendron collection. Vivid red and scarlet, orange and crimson were not allowed to swamp the pastel colours, pinks and blues, and the yellows, which were a particular favourite of Sir Eric.

Magnolias, much loved by the Queen Mother, were planted in those early days with an eye to the future, and that future has now come with magnificent species like the clear pink *Magnolia campbellii*; the rose-purple *M. c.* ssp. *mollicomata*; a bright pink cross between *M. c.* and *M. c.* ssp. *mollicomata*, which from a seedling flowered in thirteen years, was named 'Charles Raffill' and was awarded an Award of Merit in 1963 and First Class Certificate in 1966; *M. sargentiana* var. *robusta*; *M. sprengeri*; *M. dawsoniana*; *M. kobus* and the Japanese willow-leaf magnolia, *M. salicifolia; M. denudata* and *M.* x *veitchii*.

Rising out of a sea of green, and in some cases against a background of conifers, these now mature trees are a breathtaking sight in the early and late spring.

A truly exotic touch was added by the Chilean flameflower *(Embothrium coccineum)* raised from seed collected high in the mountains of Chile by Dr. Wilfrid Fox.

The Totem Pole was present
in 1958 to Her Majesty the
Queen to celebrate the
centenary of British Columb

The Obelisk mirrored in the water

Three years after the first planting began, the Valley Gardens acquired the Stevenson collection of species rhododendrons from Tower Court, Ascot, at that time regarded as the most comprehensive collection in the world. It comprised two thousand plants and four hundred and sixty species.

John Barr 'Jack' Stevenson was one of this century's outstanding rhododendron experts. In 1918 he began putting together his remarkable collection which he used in his work to classify and group the species into series and sub-series, and by planting them in their appropriate groups created what was nothing less than a living reference library of rhododendrons, and out of this came most of the information contained in the Rhododendron Society's book *The Species Rhododendron*, which he edited in 1930.

The species came from the impeccable source of the seed collected in the wild. Sowing, pricking out and planting were the tasks that he shared with his wife, Roza, who was part Danish and a former ballet dancer. Someone who knew her well described her as 'a darling person', and certainly she was as devoted to the collection as was her husband.

In a letter to Lanning Roper, the author of *The Gardens in The Royal Park at Windsor*, she explained how the collection came about and its purpose.

'Because of the muddle within the genus Rhododendron and the general lack of knowledge of the hundreds of new species sent back by the collectors in the field within a comparatively few years, my husband became convinced that much could be learned by grouping them in our gardens by series. Gradually as this vision became reality, he evolved the plan for a book embodying these same principles. Thus out of our collection of living species, meticulously grown under name and collector's number and arranged by series and sub-series, the important record entitled *The Species Rhododendron* took shape and it finally appeared as edited by my husband. The plants at Tower Court were shifted when necessary to conform to the arrangement of series as laid down therein, and the Tower Court collection became the "book in being".

'The book itself, as pointed out in my husband's preface, was inevitably imperfect and incomplete, and just as Dr. Macqueen Cowan and Mr. H.H. Davidian have seen fit to alter series by regrouping and even by "sinking" species where several were too close to their botanical characteristics for adequate differentiation on the part of horticulturists, so it was necessary to alter the groupings by series of the actual plants. How fortunate it is that rhododendrons as a genus are essentially shallow-rooted plants and do not mind disturbance from time to time as moving becomes essential because of overcrowding and to preserve the planting by series.'

The fact that rhododendrons can be moved at any time and size was to prove the saviour of this great collection.

In 1950 Jack Stevenson died, and Roza Stevenson found herself with a large house, garden, staff, the unique collection, and very little money to support them. She was obliged to pull down the house and replace it with a smaller and more manageable one, but she could not afford to maintain and manage the collection, which by this time had become overcrowded and was in need of constant attention.

To destroy the collection in the interests of economy was unthinkable, and to sell it piecemeal would see it broken up for ever, and thus a loss to horticulture and botany,

he beauty of bark: River Birch,
veet Chestnut, Silver Birch

as well as the dispersal of a unique gene bank, which was equally unthinkable. But sell it she must. Mrs. Stevenson put it on the market in its entirety, which made finding a buyer extremely difficult.

Top: Narcissus bulbocodium citrin

Bottom: Narcissus cyclamineus

Overleaf: A host of golden daffodils: the Lenten lily

Jack Stevenson was a close gardening friend of King George VI. He had given many fine plants to both the Savill and Valley Gardens, had selected the spot for the famous Punch Bowl Kurume azaleas, and provided the cuttings from the original stock collected by E.H. Wilson in Japan. When the king heard that the species collection was up for sale he immediately recognised that the home for it was the Valley Gardens. He and Sir Eric decided that the ideal site for it were the eastern and southern slopes of Breakheart Hill.

However, the Crown Commissioners, presumably on instruction from the Treasury, ruled that the eleven thousand pounds being asked for the collection in 1949 was too great for a country still reeling from the cost of six years of war. Sir Eric passed on the bad news to the king, who managed to persuade the then chancellor of the exchequer, Hugh Gaitskell, to sanction the money.

By 1950 the acquisition was completed and work began on clearing the site, which now covers sixty acres. The best of the natural forest trees were left to provide shelter and a canopy, while the rest were felled and the stumps rooted out to discourage the growth of honey fungus in the rotting wood.

The preparation of the site was an enormous undertaking. After the tree felling and scrub clearance, bulldozers were used to create the Great Ride, which to start with was to be the highway for the trucks and trailers bringing in the rhododendrons, many of which were large mature plants. The only way to rid the site of its huge matted colony of bracken was to dig it out by hand, after which the thin, sandy soil was reinforced with leaf-mould and peat, which was trenched into the planting sites. Every year since then the beds have been mulched with leaf-mould, which is now so deep that the soil is springy underfoot. Mulch is a religion in both the Savill and Valley Gardens, and, indeed, is essential when gardening on thin, sharp draining, sandy soil. The evidence that it works is to be seen wherever you look in the two gardens in the superb quality of the plants.

Under the acquisition agreement the collection had to be removed from Tower Court by the spring of 1954, with the vacated land levelled and left ready for landscaping. In fact the transfer had to be extended and was not completed until the end of 1956, although the first removals, the arboreum series, began in the autumn of 1951.

Because the rhododendrons would be far more exposed to harsh winter weather in the Valley Gardens than at Tower Court, plant collectors like Frank Kingdon-Ward, Joseph Rock, Frank Ludlow and George Sherriff, all of whom had very considerable first-hand knowledge of the species growing in their natural habitat, and the weather conditions they endured, were consulted on the positioning of the different species, and their advice was followed by Sir Eric and Hope Findlay, and particularly by William Hunt, the senior gardener who had come to Windsor early in 1949, and was put in charge of 'Operation Transplant', heading a gang of six men.

Every morning Hunt and his team went to Tower Court to lift plants. Anyone who has lifted large specimen rhododendrons, trees or shrubs will know that it is not a

p: The Valley Gardens take ape: initial clearing in the ain Valley, February 1946

ttom: The arrival of the Tower ourt *Rhododendron* Species llection

simple matter of digging them up.

After tying in the branches, the extent of the root system has to be established, which is not too difficult in the case of largely surface rooting plants like rhododendrons. After that a deep trench is dug all round the specimen, the root ball is excavated, as much surplus soil as possible removed without damaging the roots, and the whole mass has to be tilted so that bagging material can be worked under the ball and around it to protect it during transit.

Once all this had been done, the Tower Court plants, many of them weighing many hundredweights, had to be manhandled out of the excavation and loaded on to a truck or a trailer for the eight-mile journey to Breakheart Hill. The largest and heaviest of these was a specimen of *Rh. falconeri*, which was fourteen feet tall, with a spread of over eighteen feet, and weighed one and a half tons. It took two hours to get it to its destination. Telephone wires had to be lifted to get it under them, and other vehicles on the road were forced to drive on to the verges as it made its stately progress.

The lifted plants were stored in a holding area with their root balls further protected with leaves. Every two weeks, under the supervision of Sir Eric and Hope Findlay, the plants were set out where they were to be planted, along with the other trees and shrubs arranged amongst them to create diversity and interest.

Owners of many of the great gardens around Windsor and elsewhere gave Sir Eric a free hand to collect propagating material from their own collections of plants.

The largest rhododendrons were left out on the handcarts which has been used to haul them out of the excavations so that they were as undisturbed as possible in the holding area.

In some cases planting was almost as difficult as the lifting, since the planting sites were on steep slopes. So that the rhododendrons would not be at an angle and in danger of being toppled down the slope by any erosion caused by heavy falls of rain, small circular terraces had to be built from soil and turves.

By the spring of 1953 a thousand plants of the arboreum, cinnabarinum, neriiflorum, thomsonii, grande, falconeri, triflorum and azalea series had been moved into the Valley Gardens. By December 1956 the number had increased to two thousand, including the trichocladum and micranthum series. Over that period there were only fifty casualties.

A great deal was learned about the effect of moving mature rhododendrons. Some went on strike and refused to flower for a considerable period, while others were stimulated into excessive flowering as though they were performing a swan song. One reason for the survival success rate must be put down to the massive amount of leaf-mould worked into the soil. No artificial fertilisers were used.

Transferring the rhododendron species collection was probably the last great movement of mature plants ever likely to take place in Britain. Such a lengthy, labour intensive operation would not be economically viable. The whole collection would be vegetively reproduced by layering, grafting and cuttings, with the parent plants being uprooted and destroyed. Had this happened the collection would have taken a great many years to become established. In fact, as well as being moved, the species were also

Stately Scots pines: a vital element in the Valley Garden

Overleaf: The Cascade at the head of Virginia Water

vegetively reproduced to allow for losses.

In the decades since the collection was established in its new home it has proved its worth by providing the parents for the internationally famous Windsor hybrids, which have been formed into a collection on their own planted between the Punch Bowl and the Azalea Valley.

Much of the development and success of the Valley Gardens was due to the skill of an outstanding gardener, John 'Bob' Elcock.

Another truly amazing rhododendron collection is that of Kurume azaleas massed in a horseshoe curve at the top end of the Punch Bowl, which is a natural amphitheatre, and the perfect setting for the truly spectacular display of colour they put on in May each year.

The Punch Bowl is a semicircular amphitheatre stretching from east to west, and is open to the south and the sun, while at the same time being sheltered. The slope where the Kurumes are planted drops about forty feet to the floor of the amphitheatre.

These neat evergreen rhododendrons, which could have been designed specifically for small modern gardens, were introduced from Japan to America in 1916 and 1920 by E.H. Wilson, the British-born plant collector, who was then living in America working and collecting for the Arnold Arboretum in Boston, Massachusetts.

In 1914 Wilson had seen a number of the dwarf rhododendrons in a nursery outside Tokyo, where he had been told that they had been raised by a Japanese nurseryman, Motozo Sakamoto, early in the nineteenth century at Kurume on the southern island of Kyushu. It was to the city of Kurume that Wilson travelled in the spring of 1918 to the nursery of Kijiro Akashi, who had inherited the Sakamoto collection, and had then spent the next forty years hybridising them. When Wilson met him he had no less than two hundred and fifty hybrids, and from these Wilson selected fifty to take home to America. Of that fifty he declared six to be outstanding – 'Takasago', cherry blossom pink; 'Azuma Kagami', deep pink; 'Kirin', deep rose; 'Kumo-no-uye', pure salmon; 'Kurai-no-himo', carmine; and the white 'Kureno-yuki'.

He also went to the source of the Kurume, Kirishima, the sacred mountain in the south of Japan, where Sakamoto had collected his parent plants from among the very variably coloured species that grew there. When Wilson arrived the slopes were a brilliant mass of colour: red, white, magenta, salmon, mauve and pink.

Overwhelmed by the rhododendrons he dubbed them 'The Princess Kurume', and in his book *Plant Hunting* he might have had this adulatory passage dictated by fellow collector, Reginald Farrer, who was famous for his florid prose: 'We have the honor (sic) to announce that Princess Kurume, reigning beauty of the Azalea Kingdom, is in town and will hold court throughout Easter. Further, I have to declare the Princess' intention of becoming a permanent resident, also, that in each succeeding year her court will be held continuously from Christmas to Easter. The doors are open to all. Her handsome debonair Chinese cousin, under the pseudonym Indian Azalea, has been long a favorite (sic) in the floral courts of America and Europe and so, too, have other relatives, but endowed with radiant beauty this youthful, winsome Princess is bound to capture and hold the stronghold of public affection and esteem. She first came to these shores as a baby in 1916 and in 1920 a few favored (sic) folk were

permitted to peep at this charming damsel in conservative Boston, Massachusetts. The effect was magical, all who saw her forthwith became her devotees. Her first lover in this part of the world, her sponsor and guardian, I immediately found myself a mere atom in her universe.'

Magnolia x *loebneri* 'Merrill'

In 1946 Jack Stevenson, who was closely involved in the Valley Gardens from its inception, pointed out the Punch Bowl as the ideal spot for planting a collection of Kurume azaleas, and undertook to provide the propagating material from his collection of 'Wilson's Fifty'. The cuttings were made by Adrian Ellis, one of the most outstanding propagators to work in the gardens.

While the stock was being built up the area was cleared of an over-growth of larches, and once again the bracken was dug out by hand. A series of paths like tracks in the side of a ravine were cut out so that now the Kurumes in all their glory can be seen from the top and in various stages down until you reach the floor of the amphitheatre.

The original fifty varieties were quite quickly reduced to thirty-eight when twelve were found to be too tender to survive. The remainder thrive on an annual mulch of leaf-mould and a trim which takes off the seed pods but encourages sideshoots, which is why they always look so compact.

Rivalling the Kurumes for colour are the plants in the Azalea Valley with its collections of Ghent and Mollis hybrids, the Knaphill-Exbury strains, the national collection of Glenn Dale rhododendrons (azaleas), and the great thickets of gloriously scented *Rh. luteum,* once known as *Azalea ponticum.*

It would be wrong to go away with the idea that the Valley Gardens are an exclusive enclave of rhododendrons. This superb forest garden has been planted with a huge range of shrubs and ornamental trees, most prominent among them being camellias, sorbus, cherries (prunus), pieris, amelanchier, magnolias, mahonia, hydrangea, acer, an extensive collection of conifers, including a coppice of the dawn redwood (*Metasequoia glyptostroboides*), the handkerchief tree (*Davidia involucrata*), willows (salix), corylopsis, species roses, the flannel or calico bush (*Kalmia latifolia*), hamamelis, viburnums, stewartia, the Persian ironwood (*Parrotia persica*), the golden rain tree (*Koelreuteria paniculata*), the burnt sugar tree (*Cercidiphyllum japonicum*), photinia, fothergilla and cotoneaster to say nothing of the spring glory of literally acres of naturalised *Narcissus pseudonarcissus, N. bulbocodium citrinus* and *N. cyclamineus.*

The origin of the spectacular sheets of *N. bulbocodium citrinus* and *N. cyclamineus* were a couple of packets of seed collected by Frank Waley, an outstanding expert on narcissi. Both before and after the war he collected seed in Spain, Portugal and North Africa. The seed he gave to the Windsor gardens was sown directly where it was to grow in the damp 'alpine' meadow in the Valley Gardens, which is very similar to a Spanish alpine meadow, except that it is only one hundred feet, and not thousands of feet, above sea level.

Every year when the seed pods are full they are collected (it is a hands and knees job), cleaned, and sown into the grass in June. Exactly the same is done with the *N. pseudonarcissus.*

Although the narcissi in the Savill Garden are not as breathtaking as those in the

Valley Gardens, they are also naturalised, along with *Crocus tommasinianus*, which is extremely variable in colour from silvery lilac to almost pink.

The spring and early summer are, of course, a brilliant period in the Valley Gardens, but the winter is certainly not without colour. One of the loveliest sights is *Mahonia* x *media* 'Charity' sporting its crests of bright yellow fragrant flowers. Probably one of the most popular of all mahonias, it owes its existence to Sir Eric's instinct for a good plant.

He paid a visit to the Windlesham Nurseries of John Russell looking for six *Mahonia lomarifolia*. When he examined the quite tiny plants on offer he spotted three rogue plants. He bought them along with the lomarifolia. One of the rogues turned out to be 'Charity', a cross between *M. lomarifolia* and *M. japonica*. Another cultivar from the same cross, 'Lionel Fortescue', named after the creator of the Garden House at Buckland Monochorum in Devon, won Fortescue the Reginald Cory Memorial Cup.

Between the rhododendron species collection and Azalea Valley there is the national holly (ilex) collection, which can be easily overlooked in the summer when the berries have gone and the foliage takes on a kind of matt finish, but in the winter it becomes bright, polished and colourful.

Also in many ways at its best in the winter is the Heather Garden just across the road from Smith's Lawn on the eight-acre site of what had been sand pits and heath land. Not only does it contain a superb collection of heaths (erica), St. Dabeoc's heath (daboecia) and ling (calluna), but also dwarf conifers and a wide range of ericaceous plants.

It took about six years to prepare and plant thirty-six years ago. Because the planting followed the tortuous natural contours which include shallow pits and big lumpy hummocks, the whole effect is of a piece of natural scrubland, with something of interest at every twist and turn.

There is only one building in the Valley Gardens, and that is the pavilion built as a memorial to Lord Plunket, who was Master of the Household, and himself a great gardener.

It is a very calm and peaceful place in which to sit.

But then that can be said of the whole of the Valley Gardens, and it reminds me of the song that Amiens sings in the Forest of Arden in Shakespeare's *As You Like It:*

'Under the greenwood tree,
Who loves to lie with me,
And turn his merry note
Unto the sweet bird's throat,
Come hither, come hither, come hither.
Here shall he see no enemy
But winter and rough weather.'

ıe Plunket Memorial

verleaf: The Canadian Avenue
ıs presented to the estate by
e Canadian Lumber Corps
hich was stationed in the
reat Park during the 1914–18
ar

from Japan in 1937 for nine old pennies each. Near by a *Rh. barbatum* hybrid is a beacon of deep red.

Even more joyously alive and colourful is the Heather Garden, particularly the gentle mound of mixed *erica* x *darleyensis* cultivars; 'Jack H. Brummage', 'Furzey', 'Ghost Hills', 'Arthur Johnson', 'Jenny Porter', 'J.W. Porter', 'Darley Dale', 'Silberschmelze', 'George Rendall' and 'White Perfection' combining in an exquisite quilt of soft tones of pinks, purples, mauves, reds and white, the gentle soothing colours of a medieval tapestry.

And where colour is missing it is replaced at this time of the year with the penetrating, seductive scent of flowers you have to search for, like the demure little tufty white blooms that hide themselves under the leaves of the Christmas box (*Sarcococca hookeriana* var. *humilis*), and the yellow-green clusters of *Lindera obtusiloba.*

From early April there is absolutely no doubt that spring has arrived in the Valley Gardens. The magnolias are opening their stars and goblets, and you pray that a sharp frost will not transform their purity to soggy, brown, blasted petals.

The star magnolia (*M. stellata*) is beginning to shine, particularly the pure white cultivar 'Royal Star', and a pretty pink form which is underplanted with Solomon's seal (polygonatum), as well as the starry white *M.* 'Grayswood' (x *loebneri* seedling). The large white cups, often stained with purple of *M.* x *soulangiana* are just beginning to open, and so are the deep pink flowers of *M.* 'Charles Raffill'.

Pieris japonica 'Flamingo' is a mass of deep pink lily of the valley flowers. The young leaves of *Acer palmatum* 'Katsura' are a burnt orange-red, and the pale yellow flowers of *Corylopsis glabrescens* fills the air with the spicy fragrance of orange zest. Suddenly you come across a golden glow which is a thicket of *Forsythia* x *intermedia*, which is a cross between *F. suspensa* and *F. viridissima*, and the cerise pink of a cherry, *Prunus* 'Shosar' (*P. campanulata* x *P. sargentii*).

Acres of the Valley are now awash with narcissus. A great drift of the Lenten lily (*N. pseudonarcissus*) covers the ground in the copse of dawn redwood (*Metasequoia glyptostroboides*), which was grown from seed collected in China just after the Second World War. It was a tree long thought to have been extinct, and only to be found in fossil form. In 1941 it was found alive and thriving in eastern Sichuan and western Hubei, where it had been grown for as long as anyone could remember to protect riverbanks and paddy fields from being damaged by floods, and was known as the Chinese water fir.

Millions of the little *N. bulbocodium citrinus* and *N. cyclamineus* dye the hollows and slopes lemon yellow and gold.

This is the spring and the season of the rhododendrons. It starts gently enough with big trusses of pale yellow flowers flushed with pink of a specimen of the Grande series, and the sulphur-yellow flowers of *Rh.* 'Golden Oriole' (*moupinense* x *sulphureum*), set off against the peeling cinnamon bark. There are huge trusses of pink bells of *Rh. sutchuenense*, with dark speckling and a magenta throat.

By the middle of April there is a glorious eruption of rhododendron flowers, bells and trumpets, and vast, opulent clusters, some in pure and flawless colours, others delicately stippled, spotted and blotched as though an artist had decided to enhance

ɔposite: "Pepperpot" planting
Erica x darleyensis cultivars

p: *Rh. yunnanense* and the
thor

ɔttom: *Pieris japonica*
'rayswood'

Magnolias: a March scene

their beauty in an abstract way.

The way to see this remarkable collection is to wander through it in an abstracted kind of way and let whatever takes your eye hold your eye.

There from Korea is the bright mauve-pink of *Rh. mucronulatum*, and not so far away *Rh. irroratum* 'Polka Dot', with its pale pink flowers pepper-potted with purple spots. Then there are two collections of *Rh. rubiginosum* YU. 821688 and F. 21348, both from southern China, the first pale violet and the second a deeper rose violet. It is just such a group as this which makes the collection so important by demonstrating how variable these wonderful plants are.

Also from southern China is the soft pink *Rh. lukiangense* R. 11357, and then the rose-pink trusses of *Rh. fulvum* Farrer 874, which has upright leaves like hare's ears showing the cinnamon indumentum. Also pale pink, but with a rich purple throat is *Rh. fulvum* F. 24314 – fulvoides type. In a pleasing contrast are the small trusses of white flowers flushed with rose-violet of *Rh. heliolepis* var. *brevistylum* MCL. D. 148.

Against all these soft colours the blue of *Rh. campanulatum* 'Stonefield' stands out, and although they are large they have a job to compete with the magnificent trusses of the great Himalayan giants, *Rh. sinogrande*, with its huge pale yellow flowers with their scarlet throats in loose clusters, and perhaps the most wonderous of all rhododendrons, *Rh. macabeanum*, collected in Manipur by Frank Kingdon-Ward, with its primrose yellow corollas, with a purple-black throat.

But the beauty of this collection is that it shows just how rich and diverse the rhododendrons are, and what makes it of great value is the fact that the species carry the collectors' numbers, which makes them an invaluable source of reference. There are the pink buds opening to white bells of the *williamsianum* hybrid *Rh.* 'Pook'; the daffodil-yellow *Rh.* 'Remo', and the pale yellow tubes, flushed with rose-pink of *Rh.* 'Crossbill' (*lutescens* x *spinuliferum*). A bank looks like a lava flow from the dark red flowers of *Rh.* 'Jenny' (*forrestii* x *griersonianum*) tumbling down the slope, and there is even deeper red from *Rh. sanguineum* ssp. *consanguineum* R. 10900.

It is almost a relief to move away from this feast of rhododendrons and be soothed by the pink and white of magnolias among a setting of dark green conifers. The conifers are worth examining closely, particularly gems like *Chamaecyparis lawsoniana* Elegantissima', with its soft cascading foliage just touched with cream.

Looking out on this flowering forest scene it is almost impossible to believe that in October 1987 thousands of fully mature trees were felled in a few hours by a hurricane.

Down by the still sheet of Virginia Water a little boggy cove is clogged with the bold and brassy skunk cabbage (*Lysichiton americanus*) spathes framed by alders and rhododendrons.

Although it has yet to put on its grand display, the Punch Bowl is fringed with pink and white camellias, pieris and magnolias, against a background of oak, birch and conifers.

In the Heather Garden the leaf buds are breaking on the southern beeches (nothofagus), and the cascading branches of the weeping beech, *Betula pendula* 'Youngii'. There are plumy tufts of buds on the tree heathers. *Erica carnea* 'March

Top: Lysichiton americanus

Bottom: Rh. x 'Loderi King George'

Overleaf left: A spring walk

Overleaf right: Rh. 'Olive'

Seedling' has created pools of pink in contrast to the pure white of *E. c.* 'Springwood White', while the heart-leaf manzanita from California (*Arctostaphylos andersonii* var. *pajaroensis* 'Paradise') is covered with pink bells and flaking green bark.

It is May, and the new leaves of the acers are red, green and gold. In the Punch Bowl there is a soft haze of colour over the Kurume azaleas as their flower buds begin to break. The ground under the trees in the beech copse behind the Punch Bowl is green with tens of thousands of beech seedlings, and just beyond the trees the 'orchard' of ornamental cherries is a foaming mass of pink and white blossom. With the leaf buds breaking the birch trees look as though they are dusted with pale green.

Amelanchiers are coming into flower in the Heather Garden, and the ione manzanita (*Arctostaphylos myrtifolia*) is smothered in pink bells. There is purslane growing under the birch trees. Amongst the heaths, berberis are lighting up the garden; *Berberis* x *stenophylla* 'Etna' is in golden bud, while *B. linearifolia* 'Orange King' is a brilliant splash of deep orange, and there are the stiff spikes of intense gold flowers of *B.* x *lologensis* 'Mystery Fire' (*darwinii* x *linearifolia*). In contrast is the pale yellow of *Mahonia piperiana*, and the almost shocking pink of the dwarf Russian almond (*Prunus tenella* var. *gessleriana*).

The x *darleyensis* cultivars are still fresh and colourful, while *Erica* x *veitchii* 'Gold Tips' is like white spindrift. *Sorbus aria* 'Lutescens' and *S. barthea* are in leaf and bud, as is the enchanting little elder-leaved *S. sambucifolia* from Japan. The leaves of *S. thibetica* 'John Mitchell' look as though they have been cut out of silver grey velvet. One of the most curiously attractive shrubs growing amongst the heather is the bitter orange (*Poncirus trifoliata*) with its angular spiked twigs and large white flowers.

Even more rhododendrons are now in flower. *Rh. williamsianum*, one of the parents of so many superb hybrids, has its neat heart-shaped leaves draped with pink bells. *Rh. campylocarpum* ssp. *caloxanthum* has fully opened its pale yellow bells. Also bell-shaped are the creamy-yellow flowers, held in huge clusters, of *Rh. falconeri* from northern India. The deep pink of 'Thomwilliams' (*thomsonii* x *williamsianum*) contrast perfectly with the oxalis and lily of the valley growing under it, and so do the enormous trusses of the ivory white flowers of *Rh. basilicum*, from southern China, and the underplanting of Solomon's seal.

There is a soft fragrance from the large pale yellow flowers of *Rh.* 'Princess Margaret' ('Hawk Crest' x *loderi* 'Julie'). On another cross of the same two varieties the blooms are ivory.

In the most striking contrast are the glowing red of *Rh.* 'J.G. Millais' ('Ascot Brilliant' x 'Pink Pearl'), and the orange-red buds, which open to lemon yellow, of *Rh.* 'Clewer' (*litiense* x 'Hawk Crest'). There is a luminous glow of pink from *Rh.* 'Kiev' x yakushimanum, and the Kingdon-Ward collected *Rh. tephropelum* K-W. 13006 from south-west China is practically jangling with tiny pink bells.

The bold scarlet of *Rh.* (*forrestii* var. *repens* x 'Aries' x *neriiflorum*), and *Rh. neriiflorum* itself, combine splendidly with the golden-amber of *Rh.* 'Alison Johnstone' (*concatenans* x *yunnanense*), and the white of *Rh.* 'Colonel Rogers' (*falconeri* x *niveum*), both of which are flushed with pink.

By the middle of the month the huge pink flowers of *Rh.* x *loderi* are scenting the

rbus 'Savill Orange'

Valley Gardens, and there are big blue trusses on *Rh. campanulatum* 'Graham Thomas', banana yellow flowers of *Rh. keiskei* from Japan, those of *Rh.* 'Viscy' ('Diane' x *viscidifolium)* are a lovely shade of yellow overlaid with pink, while the groups of *Rh. yakushimanum* are a foaming mass of bloom.

But it is not all rhododendrons. The enkianthus are displaying their pretty little bells, while the bracts of *Cornus nuttalli* 'Monarch' are huge and green-white. The young bracts of the handkerchief tree (*Davidia involucrata*) are still flushed with green, but soon they will be pure white and this superb Chinese tree will be at its most magnificent. Some of them in the Valley Gardens have clusters of mistletoe growing from the branches. The birches are dripping with catkins.

In the area between the Pinetum Valley and the Azalea Valley, the thickets of *Rh. luteum (Azalea luteum)* flood the whole area with an almost overwhelming scent a little like honeysuckle. It has been grown in Britain since 1793, when it was introduced either from the Caucasus or Turkey where it grows wild. Within a few years of its introduction, under the name of both *Azalea pontica* and *Rh. flavum*, it was being used as a parent of crosses with the North American species, and is, indeed, the mother of most of the modern hybrids.

This is a sight and a scent not to be missed in the gardens, made all the more beautiful by the bluebells and pink campion growing freely among the bushes.

Although, year by year, weather conditions play a major part in the flowering of the Kurume azaleas in the Punch Bowl, usually by the last week or ten days of May they are at their best.

It is hard to adequately describe the Kurume at their peak of perfection. It is something that has to be seen. It is exuberant, exotic, vivid and dramatic. It is like a vast cape embroidered with huge abstract splashes of red, pink, lilac, orange, white, flame and white flushed with pink, spread over a hillside.

Almost as brilliant are the yellow, salmon, flame and orange red of the flowers in the Azalea Valley, so that it is a relief to cool your eyes on the foaming white blossom of the lovely crab apple (*Malus hupehensis*), and the cushions of white flushed with pink of *Rh. yakushimanum*, and those of *Rh.* 'Hydon Dawn' (*yakushimanum* x 'Springbok') fading to a rose pink. The multi-colours of the yakushimanum hybrid collection are softened by the underplanting of the golden-leaved *Hosta fortunei* 'Aurea', and the pale blue-green of *H. tokudama*.

The sheer voluptuousness and extravagance of the spring and early summer colour in the gardens subsides gently from mid summer, but it is simply the forest garden taking a rest before staging its great and gorgeous autumn display of colour and rich fruits.

As an overture there are the stewartia and eucryphia in flower, and the magnificent banks of hydrangea. A single hydrangea bush reminds one of the dusty front garden of a seaside boarding house, but grown in great sweeps and clumps they are superb. Clearly it is how they should be grown, and how they are in the Valley Gardens.

There are snow drifts of *Hydrangea macrophylla* 'Lanarth White', and the spring sky blue of *H. m.* 'Générale Vicomtesse de Vibraye'. *H. m.* 'Blue Wave' is a sea of electric blue, while *H. m.* 'Taube' is a much deeper shade, and *H. m.* 'Blue Deckle' the pale blue

Ƭhe autumn splendour of
apanese maples

of a clear winter sky.

By September the white bracts of *H. paniculata* are turning pink, while the sterile flowers of *H. villosa* are pale purple, with the stamens on the fertile flowers looking like tiny flames of intense blue, and there are the pastel shades of *H. p.* 'Unique' and *H. p.* 'Pink Diamond', and the pure white of *H. p.* 'Kyushu', which was given an Award of Merit in 1964.

Although only late flowering varieties of rhododendrons like 'Polar Bear' (*diaprepes* x *auriculatum*), which was bred by Stevenson at Tower Court, and those that have fooled themselves into believing that spring has come early, are in bloom, the silver and cinnamon indumentum on the undersides of the leaves of many of the species seems more pronounced as the autumn and winter approach.

The foliage of *Cornus* 'Eddie's White Wonder' (*florida* x *nuttalli*) First Class Certificate 1977, which won the Reginald Cory Cup for the gardens in 1972, is turning bright with autumn colour, and the strawberry fruits of *C. kousa* are like pendant rubies. The spiny fruit cases of the sweet chestnuts look like lime-green sea urchins, and the huge cylinder seed capsules of *Rh. sinogrande* are covered with a velvety indumentum like the velvet on the horns of young deer.

Throughout the gardens, foliage is blazing into colour like small forest fires. *Hamamelis mollis* is butter yellow, and *H.* x *intermedia* 'Arnold Promise' (*japonica* x *mollis*), bright orange and gold. Cherry leaves are like hot embers, while those of *Rh. luteum* are tongues of flame.

Maples (acer) are doing what they do best, turning the drab green of summer into rainbow ribbons. Close to the rhododendron species collection there is a towering acer now shrimp pink and gold. The small grape leaves of *Acer japonicum* 'Vitifolium' are gold, yellow, red and pink. *A. palmatum* 'Osakazuki' is burgundy red, and *A. p.* 'Sango Kaku' (syn. 'Senkaki') is a mass of the most beautiful gold and pink.

A. griseum is gracefully shedding its bark to reveal the polished cinnamon new bark underneath, and it is dripping with pale green-white keys (seeds). Rather in the way that we tend to overlook the beauty of acer flowers, so we tend to ignore their lovely seeds. Those of *A. p.* 'Osakazuki' are deep rose-pink.

Under the trees and shrubs the ferns are still green and graceful in the early autumn, but before long they will become russet and rusty, gold and brown.

Sorbus are full of fruit. The mountain ash (*Sorbus aucuparia*), with its crowded clusters ranging from sealing wax red to deep orange, is rather more generous than the whitebeams (*S. aria*), which, although the fruit is larger, tend not to be overloaded, but there is great charm in their deeply coloured fruits peeping out from among large grey-green leaves, and perhaps there is no sorbus with greater charm than the combination of both, the oak-leaved *Sorbus* x *thuringiaca (aria* x *aucuparia)*, with its pillar-box red berries.

The brilliance of the Punch Bowl has become shades of green illuminated with the colouring leaves of acers and the strobili of cedar coated in pale yellow pollen. Photinia are studded with grenadier-red berries, and in the bottom of the bowl the vast leaves of a great group of *Gunnera manicata* are the deep, dark green they become before collapsing for the winter.

Top: Hydrangea paniculata 'Pink Diamond'

Bottom: Sorbus cashmiriana

THE GRASS MEN

'he National Collection of
warf and slow-growing
onifers

Without Sir Eric Savill, his successor, John Bond, and the gardeners, such as the charge hand, William 'Bill' Shefford, who have dedicated their working lives to them, there would be no Savill and Valley Gardens. Equally there would have been precious little to put into them but for the tenacity, genius, raw courage, and a very special aesthetic sense for exceptional beauty in the flora of the world, of that extraordinary, and often eccentric group of people – the plant hunters.

The search for new plants has occupied the energies of mankind since hunter gatherers began digging up roots, bulbs and tubers, picking fruits and nuts, and harvesting greenery and grain to go with the wild meat they hunted. As the centuries advanced the quest became more sophisticated and selective. The ancient Egyptians were ever on the look out for plants that would render aromatic incenses for their elaborate temple ceremonies; the Greeks and Romans were interested in fruits and vegetables to expand their already very diverse diet, as well as flowers, which they valued for their scent as well as their beauty.

As now, the search for medicinal herbs to cure disease and relieve pain, was always a priority, as well as economic plants for timber, fibres and dyes.

Plant hunting and collecting came late to Britain. The Roman conquerors introduced their favourite fruits, vegetables and other crops. Little or nothing arrived during the Dark Ages, and what was cultivated was kept alive in the physic and kitchen gardens and orchards of religious houses by monks and nuns.

Castles, which were at the heart of landowning, offered little scope for ornamental gardening, except very small privy gardens. It was not until the castles gave way to palaces and manor houses that gardening became a truly serious occupation of the wealthy, and with it the demand for new and exotic plants. It was out of that demand that plant collecting grew.

Being great gardens, the Savill and Valley Gardens contain plants which represent the majority of the famous British collectors of the past three hundred and fifty years.

Among the first and keenest aristocratic gardeners was Sir Robert Cecil, the first Lord Salisbury, who early in the seventeenth century sent John Tradescant, his gardener, to scour France and Holland for rarities and curiosities for the gardens of Hatfield House. Tradescant went on to collect in North Africa and Russia, and his son, John the Younger, made important collections in Virginia and the West Indies.

Although not their original collections, there are Tradescant plants to be found in the Gardens, not least a magnificent London plane (*Platanus* x *acerifolia*), thought to be a cross between *Platanus orientalis* and *P. occidentalis* which John the Elder grew in his south Lambeth garden in London. The seed of *P. occidentalis* was collected by his son, and the famous pollution resistant London plane was a seedling which appeared in the garden.

The first collector appointed by the Royal Botanic Gardens, Kew, Francis Masson, is represented in the Savill Garden's Temperate House with fine plants of the bird of paradise flower (*Strelitzia reginae*) which he introduced from South Africa in the late eighteenth century. Grevilleas in the house are a reminder of Alan Cunningham, sent to Australia by Kew in the early nineteenth century. Early in the same century the Royal Horticultural Society, then just the Horticultural Society, sent David Douglas to North America. He was a prolific collector, notably of conifers. Sitka spruce (*Picea sitchensis*) and its cultivars, and a long list of pines – *Pinus contorta, P. coulteri, P. lambertiana, P. monticola, P. ponderosa, P. radiata, P. sabiana* – are all to be found in the gardens, including the great Douglas fir (*Pseudotsuga menziesii*), of which there are no less than twenty-six cultivars represented.

Rh. 'Roza Stevenson'

Douglas, who withstood horrendous hardship and danger during his travels, was called the 'Grass Man' by the North American Indians, because of his apparently lunatic obsession with gathering plants. This strange behaviour of plant hunters was noted with amusement, astonishment and sometimes hostility in many parts of the world, not least in China, which was to become one of, if not, the most important collecting ground in the world for northern hemisphere gardens.

Robert Fortune, another RHS collector, effectively spearheaded the western plant exploration of China, although there must have been times when he wished he hadn't bothered. He was attacked by mobs and had to fight off Chinese pirates with a pistol and a shotgun, which the RHS had supplied on the understanding that he returned them in good order. Despite this, he collected many superb plants. The lovely cultivars of *Anemone hupehensis* in the great herbaceous border in the Savill Garden are with us thanks to his original collection of plants in a Chinese graveyard, where the white species is planted as it is the Chinese colour of mourning. These fine plants are nearly always sold as *A. japonica.*

Winter jasmine (*Jasminum nudiflorum*) is a Fortune plant, and the superb natural planting of *Forsythia* x *intermedia* in the Valley Gardens is thanks to Fortune who collected and introduced both the parents. He also made important original collections of Chinese rhododendrons and paeonias. The Valley Gardens also have plants of *Rh. fortunei*, raised from the seed he collected in 1856. Also in the Gardens is *Rh. metternichii, Rh.* x *obtusum* and *Rh. ovatum.*

In northern India, in the Indian Himalaya, Joseph Dalton Hooker, son of the then director of Kew, William Hooker, in that botanically exciting first half of the nineteenth century, collected rhododendrons mainly in Sikkim, which were to have a massive impact on rhododendron breeding in the following years. Most of his species, including the superb *Rh. arboreum*, which is really at its best in west country gardens, are at Windsor.

These trail-breakers set the pace for a truly remarkable era of plant hunting by British collectors that was to last from the first decade of the twentieth century until the final flickering of the Indian Empire. It was an era that embraced in particular the Indian Himalaya, western China, the Tibetan marches, northern Burma, Tibet itself, and Assam, and its success had a great deal to do with the writ of the British extending so far into Asia.

Another, and very important, reason for the bullish surge of interest in plant exploration came from a new generation of businessmen and industrialists, who were creating

[M]ichelia doltsopa 'Silver Cloud' in [th]e Temperate House

[O]verleaf: An April scene in the [R]hododendron Species [C]ollection

family estates and were intensely interested in the new naturalistic gardening in the style of William Robinson, which involved the use of a vast range of plants from trees and shrubs to climbers and perennials.

The leading suppliers were the great nursery gardening family of Veitch and Sons, who, at the turn of the century were hugely prosperous and in a position to employ their own collectors. One of the outstanding ones was Ernest Henry Wilson, a Gloucestershire boy, who started his horticultural career in Solihull, moved to the Birmingham Botanical Garden, and thence to Kew.

When he was at Kew the gardens were going through a financial crisis, so an arrangement was worked out with Veitch to send a Kew-trained man to China, and the man chosen was Wilson.

Veitch had been fascinated by the description of the handkerchief tree (*Davidia involucrata*) sent to the nursery by Augustine Henry, a British civil servant working for the Chinese Customs Service in western China. It appeared to be the almost perfect ornamental garden tree. Although it had first been recorded by a missionary-botanist, Father Armand David, Henry had actually seen a single specimen and was able to pinpoint it. Veitch wanted it, and Kew needed someone in that part of China to collect seeds, bulbs, plants and herbarium specimens.

Wilson, an energetic twenty-three-year-old, arrived in China in 1899, rendezvoused with Henry for his directions to the unique Davidia, and after a fairly rugged journey arrived at the spot to find the stump of a tree and a ramshackle hut built from its timber. It is hard to imagine the sheer horror of a young plant collector on his first expedition arriving at what was believed to be the last of a species to find that it was now a very dead tree. Fortunately Wilson was a determined character. He searched further into the forest and eventually found a grove of *Davidia involucrata*. Now they grow like a native in the Valley Gardens.

The handkerchief tree was the first of a whole series of outstanding garden plants that Wilson was to introduce during a remarkable career, which was tragically cut short by a fatal motoring accident.

His favourite plant was the glorious regal lily (*Lilium regale*), which he discovered in a remote Tibetan valley. On his return from collecting it he was seriously injured in a rock fall, which left him with one leg shorter than the other and what he called his 'lily limp'. Others that have enriched our gardens are *Acer griseum* and *A. davidii*, the kiwi fruit (*Actinidia chinensis*), now an important fruit crop, *Malus hupehensis*, *Clematis armandii*, *Ilex pernyi*, and, of course, the Kurume azaleas of the Punch Bowl. Altogether he introduced over one thousand species into gardens.

A contemporary of Wilson was another outstanding British collector, George Forrest; indeed it is strongly argued that he was the greatest of all collectors.

During twenty-eight years of collecting mainly in south-western China, and especially Yunnan, he gathered thirty-one thousand and fifteen specimens.

Forrest was essentially a man of the wilds. Throughout his boyhood his spare time was spent wandering the countryside around Falkirk, where he was born, studying the native plants, birds and butterflies and fishing in the streams. His brother, who was a keen amateur naturalist encouraged his interest.

cer grosseri var. hersii

verleaf left: Rh. cinnabarinum ssp. anthocodon Concatenans group -W. 5874

verleaf right: Lindera obtusiloba

next door to the Savill and Valley Gardens. His father occupied the chair of botany at the Royal Indian Engineering College, now part of Brunel University. In 1907 K-W took up a position as a junior master in the Shanghai Boys' Public School, an irksome job from which he escaped to join an American zoological expedition which took him six hundred miles up the Yangtze, and eventually into Tibet.

His first solo trip was made in 1911 as collector for A.K. Bulley, which took him to North Yunnan and Tibet. Over the next forty-six years he made twenty-two expeditions in China, Tibet, Burma, Assam and Ceylon, which he described vividly in sixteen books.

Among the thousands of plants he collected some have proved to be among the most outstanding ever to come into cultivation. He collected the first batch of seed of the blue poppy (*Meconopsis betonicifolia*), which he found in the rugged Tsangpo Gorge country in Tibet, and at the same time the pretty, scented pink turk's cap lily (*Lilium wardii*), and the last wild lily to be brought into cultivation, *L. mackliniae*.

His primulas included *P. florindae*, *P. bulleyana*, *P. alpicola* and *P. sikkimensis*, the moonlight primula. Although the blue poppy brought him instant fame, it is for his rhododendron introductions he is best known, and many of them are to be found in the gardens – *Rh. wardii*, *Rh. macabeanum*, *Rh. campylogynum*, *Rh. cinnabarinum* 'Orange Bill', *Rh. bullatum*, *Rh. triflorum*, and several varieties of *Rh. repens*.

For ten years, until his death in 1958, he was accompanied on his expeditions by his second wife, Jean, after whom he named *L. mackliniae* (her maiden name was Macklin). In 1950 they were in Assam when a violent earthquake, about 7.6 on the Richter Scale, happened. They were camped close to the epicentre, and were lucky to escape with their lives.

Contemporaries of K-W were Frank Ludlow and George Sherriff, who explored together between 1933 and 1949 in the eastern Himalaya, and were joined on one expedition by Sir George Taylor, a highly distinguished director of the Royal Botanic Garden at Kew, and an outstanding expert on meconopsis.

Ludlow and Sherriff were a plant collectors' partnership made in heaven, although their career backgrounds were so different. Ludlow was a scientist who had read botany at Cambridge under K-W's father, Prof. Marshall Ward, while Sherriff was a soldier, educated at the Royal Military Academy at Woolwich, a talented mechanic and electrician, and a superb organiser. They were both enthralled by the Himalaya and passionate naturalists.

In Bhutan and Tibet they made prodigious natural history collections, including very large numbers of plants. In all they made seven expeditions.

Among their rhododendron collections in the rhododendron species collection in the Valley Gardens are *Rh. arboreum*, *Rh. baileyi*, *Rh. campanulatum*, *Rh. ciliatum*, *Rh. cinnabarinum* var. *purpurellum*, and *Rh. glaucophyllum*.

Perhaps one of the most outstanding plants they introduced was the tree peony (*Paeonia lutea* var. *ludlowii*) with its huge clear yellow buttercup flowers.

One of the most curious and interesting of the many remarkable collectors whose plants are to be found in the Gardens is Joseph Rock, an Austrian born into the servant classes, who became an American citizen, an academic without any real

academic qualifications and a philologist who specialised in the study of obscure Asian languages.

The Pinetum in winter

The volume of his plant collections and introductions does not compare to either his contemporaries in the field or his predecessors, but he will certainly be remembered for *Sorbus* 'Joseph Rock', with its rich autumn colour and creamy gold fruits, and the somewhat rare *Paeonia suffruticosa* ssp. *rockii* (*P.* 'Joseph Rock'), with its semi-double white flowers with a deep purple-black base to the petals.

Among the rhododendrons in the species collection are *Rh. calostrotum* 'Rock's Form', *Rh. calostrotum*, *Rh. calostrotum* ssp. *keleticum*, *Rh. haematodes* ssp. *chaetomallum* and *Rh. uvarifolium*.

Rock collected for American institutions and government departments and tended to have ample money to spend on his expeditions. Consequently he travelled with great caravans of mules and servants, and always taught his Chinese cook to prepare his favourite Viennese dishes.

The expeditions lasting two or more years are over, but the search for plants, whether as ornamentals, or in the quest for new medicines, and food and other commercial plants, is far from over.

Plant collecting, very properly, is closely controlled as exploitation cuts ever deeper into the few remaining wildernesses.

But there are still collectors in whom the ardour of the old collector-explorers still burns. Men like Tony Schilling who has collected assiduously in the Nepal Himalaya and China, North America and Australia, and Roy Lancaster a plantsman, botanist, gardener and above all an exuberant enthusiast who has travelled and collected extensively in both China and Nepal. Between them, Lancaster and Schilling have helped enormously to enrich the Savill and Valley Gardens with their collections.

The collecting of new plants is important, particularly those growing in environments that are threatened by clear fell as well as slash and burn clearance, mining operations, farming and building development. It is also equally important to re-collect species and genera already introduced, for interesting variations, and to refresh the genetic pool. In the hands of experienced collectors this offers no threat to plants in the wild. The danger comes from over enthusiastic amateurs, and commercial exploitation.

Men like Schilling and Lancaster are as interested in conservation as they are in collecting, which is why so many of their discoveries go to the Savill and Valley Gardens where they will be propagated and grown as source plants as well as for their beauty.

One of the finest Lancaster introductions is *Mahonia gracilipes*, which he found on Mount Omei in Sichuan province in China. He brought back a tiny seedling from the mountain which he delivered to John Bond's kitchen table. It grows in the Temperate House, and as well as its purple and cream flowers, it has beautiful pruinose undersides to the leaves, a feature which caught the Queen's eye when she opened the Temperate House in 1995. It is also a parent with *M. confusa* to the hybrid, *M.* x *savilleana*.

Among the Lancaster collections at the gardens is *Aucuba omeiensis* L. 614, which was also delivered to the kitchen table; *Celtis bungeana* L. 450, *Euonymus bungeanus* L.

420, *Hedera napalensis* var. *sinensis* L. 555, *Hypericum pseudohenryi* L. 1029, *H. lancasteri* L. 649, *H. maclarenii* L. 863, *Lonicera deflexicalyx* L. 904, *Malus toringoides* L. 926. 'Pere David's Peach' (*Prunus davidiana*) he collected from a tree growing on the site of the old Imperial Summer Palace north west of Beijing. Another very attractive tree whose seed he collected in China is the whitebeam (*Sorbus pallescens* L. 953).

He also found two species sorbus, L. 995 and L. 1008, which are likely to be new to cultivation, and two fine viburnums (*V. ternatum* L. 734, and *V. sempervirens* L. 832). Among the many Lancaster numbers given to the gardens are *Neillia thibetica* L. 813, *Syringa yunnanensis* L. 934, *Parabenzoin trilobum* L. 1960 and *Liquidambar acalycina.*

Tony Schilling, former deputy curator in charge of the Kew Royal Botanic Garden's garden at Wakehurst Place in West Sussex, is a leading expert on the flora of Nepal, where he acted as adviser to the royal government of Nepal on the development of a national botanical garden. He has made numerous collecting trips to that lovely Himalayan kingdom, as well as Bhutan and China, and the gardens at Windsor have benefitted.

His contributions include *Populus glauca* SCHL. 2620, *Sarcococca hookeriana* SCHL. 1160, a particularly good form which won an Award of Merit, *Camellia kissii* SCHL. 2230, *Picea smithiana* SCHL. 2399–2400, *Cupressus torulosa* SCHL. 2412, 2784, *Vaccinium sikkimense* SCHL. 2528, *Berberis koehneana* var. *auramea* SCHL. 2744, *Abelia triflora* SCHL. 2415, a new sorbus species, *S. khumbuensis* SCHL. 2341, a fine form of *Bergenia purpurascens* SCHL. 2323, *Acer sterculiaceum* SCHL. 2284, and *Cotoneaster bumthangensis* SCHL. 2991. From the southern hemisphere he collected *Nothofagus cunninghamii* SCHL. 2810, a hakea species SCHL. 2833, and *Hebe subalpina* SCHL. 2998.

EPILOGUE

In Sir Eric Savill and John Bond the Savill Garden and the Valley Gardens have been particularly blessed. They gave the greater part of their careers to the gardens, not out of necessity or some sense of duty, but through an empathy, a devotion to them which has made them the outstanding places they are today, and which they must continue to be.

Sir Eric was the designer, visionary is not too extravagant a word, who could look at a wilderness and see a garden.

John Bond, the exceptional gardener, with an unflagging passion for plants and for putting together great collections. Throughout his career as Keeper of the Gardens he has been like a stamp collector, never content with just a few specimens – he must have the whole set.

Sir Eric came from a typically upper middle class background; privately educated, at ease in the society of royalty, aristocracy and the wealthy, but also with the common touch that made him such an effective leader of the workforce in the gardens, Great Park and farms of royal Windsor.

John Bond comes from a traditional gardening background. Both his grandfather and father had been head gardeners in private service. He was born into traditional gardening, and from the age of five was growing vegetables in his own small patch, as well as raising rabbits.

When he left school, gardening was the logical step, although he was not forced into it. After a short period working for his father he set out on the then classic training route. First as the boy working in the tree and shrub nursery of John Jefferies and Sons of Cirencester. After two years he was taken on as an improver at Bodnant in Wales, the great acid soil Aberconway garden, where he began his love affair with ericaceous plants.

During his national service he served with the military police, and seriously thought of a career in the civil police, but fortunately for gardening returned to Bodnant, before moving to the great Hilliers Nursery in Hampshire as propagator, growing rhododendrons, acers and mahonias, and what he calls 'all the nice things'.

During his eight years in Hampshire he became general foreman, and began the planting of the now famous Hillier Arboretum. He also fell under the influence of the late Sir Harold Hillier. 'He influenced everyone with his enthusiasm for plants, his fund of plant knowledge and plant lore,' he recalls.

Following a short spell at the well-known West Sussex woodland garden of Leonardslee, birth place of the famous loderi rhododendrons, he started his Windsor career.

He had made several visits to the Savill and Valley Gardens, was well aware of what was going on and, as he puts it 'I had my eye on it', so when an advertisement appeared for the job of assistant keeper he successfully applied for it. He arrived in January 1963 when the gardens were covered with three feet of snow, which remained on the ground until March.

For the next seven years he worked with Sir Eric, who was renowned for being a relentlessly tough task master who did not recognise the existence of second best.

'He was a very great influence on me,' John Bond says. 'His strength. His approach to things, and his whole approach to management. He also taught me how to speak to and move among royalty.'

In 1970 he became Joint Keeper of the Gardens, and five years later, Keeper of the Gardens, a job he was to discharge with great distinction until his retirement in 1997.

Like Sir Eric he demanded and got perfection, he also practised the gardening philosophy of constant rejuvenation and refurbishment, declaring that no garden can be allowed to stand still, or the landscape goes back to wilderness.

One of his most successful developments was the Dry Garden, but with his commitment to plants, he has been responsible for a huge increase in the number of plants in the gardens, and for the now very important national plant collections.

The national collections and the exceptionally high standards maintained in the Savill Garden and the Valley Gardens are what he counts among his greatest achievements.

An equally remarkable achievement is the fact that traditional and classical gardening has been maintained since the end of the Second World War, which has seen such radical changes in gardening, with the emphasis on saving labour and costs.

The fact that the two gardens are quite as superb as they are is due to maintaining the standards and skills which have over centuries made British gardening the finest in the world. For both Sir Eric and John Bond this was achieved by being 'out there and leading from the front'. For both of them the gardens were a seven days a week job.

Although both the Savill Garden and the Valley Gardens are gardens in the purest sense of the word, being a home to such a vast range of plants, all demanding very special and varied skills and expertise, they have also acquired an important scientific role as an invaluable genetic pool, and a place for the day-to-day practice of the art and craft of horticulture and gardening.

In these days when management, accountancy and politics tend to overrule the enrichment of the human spirit if some enterprise, particularly involving public money, seems unprofitable, invariably the answer is to contract its maintenance to the lowest bidder. Should this happen to the gardens, one of the finest achievements in horticulture of the twentieth century will effectively be lost.

The Savill Garden and the Valley Gardens are triumphant places. They are truly royal gardens. They are an inspiration to all gardeners. Every visit reveals a new, and often surprising, beauty. They are a splendid over-indulgence of familiar and unfamiliar plants. They are tranquility. They are happiness.

Above: Sir Eric Savill, K.C.V.C C.B.E., M.C., M.A., V.M.H., F.R.I.C.S.

Opposite: Autumn fire: *Liquidambar styraciflua*

Overleaf: Evening light on Virginia Water